Vampires

Vampires

The Un-history of the Undead

TONY THOMPSON

black dog

First published in 2010 by

black dog books

15 Gertrude Street,
Fitzroy, Vic, 3065,
Australia
Phone +61 3 9419 9406
Fax +61 3 9419 1214
dog@bdb.com.au
Please visit us at: www.bdb.com.au

Tony Thompson asserts the moral right to be identified as author of this Work.

Cover Design by Ektavo Pty Ltd
Printed and bound in Australia by Griffin Press

The paper in this book is sourced from Finland and manufactured under ISO 14001 certification from wood grown in certified forests. No old growth forest wood has been used in the manufacture of this book.

National Library of Australia Cataloguing-in-Publication entry
Thompson, Tony.
Vampires: the un-history of the undead / Tony Thompson.
9781742031316 (pbk.)
Includes index
Bibliography
Vampires--History. Vampires in literature. Vampire films. Horror films.
398.21

10 9 8 7 6 5 4 3 2 1   10 11 12 13 14 15

Image credits:
Shutterstock: Cover, pp ii–iii, 8, 40, 56–57, 130; Photolibrary: p 24 (*Vlad the Impaler*), p 85 (*Christopher Lee as Dracula*); Getty Images: p 58 (*The Borgo Pass, oil on canvas*), p 72 (*Bela Lugosi, The Vampire Count*), p 86 (*The Lost Boys*), p 102 (*Man*); Corbis: p 100 (*Blade Trinity*), p 116 (*Buffy and Dracula*), p 146 (*Twilight author Stephenie Meyer*)

black dog books would like to thank Dr Brian Wimborne, PhD., B.Sc., B. Econ. for his thorough factual check of this book.

For Joanne and Henry

Contents

IT GLOWED IN THE DARK. In 1975, there was a minor rage in my neighbourhood for small plastic models of classic horror characters. They came in lavishly illustrated boxes and stood about 20 centimetres high. My first was Dracula. I put the model together and spent a lot of time staring at it.

I remember that I was interested in his clothes; the cape in particular inspired me to wander around the house with an orange blanket on my shoulders. But the model itself glowed in the dark. Today this might seem a bit trivial, but in 1975 it was pretty great. I would draw my curtains, hold the model up to the light and then turn out the lights. The Count was illuminated.

At about the same time, someone gave me a small paperback book on the history of horror movies. It was filled with stills from early films including the classic 1931 Bela Lugosi version of *Dracula*. It included chapters on *Frankenstein, The Wolfman,* and *The Mummy*, but I was fascinated with the vampire. The other monsters seemed a bit obvious where Dracula seemed sinister. I saw the film version of *Dracula* on a chilly Saturday morning in the gymnasium of my primary school, Elkhorn Public. Some enterprising parent decided to raise money showing old horror movies and charging a dollar admission. It was big hit and the gym was packed every Saturday at 10 o'clock. This was before DVDs or YouTube so the opportunities to see these old movies were very limited. *Dracula* did not disappoint me. Years later, while studying film at university, I listened to a lecturer make fun of Bela Lugosi's acting style and the director's crude camera work. I wasn't convinced. Lugosi will always be my main vampire.

A few years later, my mother took me to see a stage version of *Dracula*. It was a gloomy production that emphasised all of the Gothic elements of the story. I can still hear Renfield's shrieks, and can see the first terrifying appearance of the vampire. I have seen many plays since but I don't think anything has thrilled and frightened me as much as Dracula did that night.

Vampires are always simmering away somewhere in popular culture. I was a teenager in the 1980s but had little interest in most of the music of the day. Music of the 1980s is now associated with cheesy synth pop bands and the odious hair-metal genre. My own musical memories of this period include a band called Bauhaus and a creepy song called *Bela Lugosi is Dead*. Another band, called The Cramps, blended horror, rockabilly, and garage punk to create a unique and somewhat unsettling sound. Many bands including The Birthday Party from Melbourne used horror iconography to create an alternative to the rather saccharine sounds of pop radio in that period.

I have never lost interest in vampire stories. In the 1990s, *Buffy The Vampire Slayer* was a popular television show. I never watched it, thinking that it sounded more like parody than a true vampire story. I have since been put straight and become a fan. Stephenie Meyer's wildly successful stories and the subsequent film versions have put vampires front and centre in popular culture once again. Purists complain that Edward is simply too good and too moral to be a vampire. They see the creature as a figure of pure evil who is bent on nothing less than the destruction of humans. While this view of the vampire is certainly well supported by stories like Bram Stoker's *Dracula*, one of the earliest vampire stories, *Varney the Vampire*, featured a main character who came to despise himself and deeply regret his bloodsucking past. At the end of this 800 page epic, Varney throws himself into a volcano to rid the world of one more vampire.

One of my purposes with this book was to present a range of vampire stories dating back to the early 1800s, and to trace the development of the story up to the present day. Writers have suggested that every age reinvents the vampire in their own image, meaning that you can learn a lot about a period in history through its vampire stories. When vampires reappeared in the 1950s, they were often from outer space or the direct result of a nuclear war. It isn't difficult to see what was on people's minds in those days. Female vampires came into vogue in the 1960s at the same time that feminism was becoming more than just an idea. What do our vampires tell us about the world we live in today?

Another idea behind this book was to put more recent vampire stories into the context of the vampire genre. I hope that readers will track down some of the stories mentioned in this book. Bram Stoker's *Dracula* remains a great read, as does Sheridan Le Fanu's *Carmilla*. All of the books that I have mentioned are easily obtainable. Most of the films are also available and I hope that readers will track down the original *Dracula* to see if it still packs a punch.

I don't know if the plastic model Dracula that I built in 1975 is still available, or if the glow-in-the-dark feature would still be of interest. I do know that the door in my imagination that the model opened more than 30 years ago is still open today. Vampires are always bigger than one writer or filmmaker. It is a story that we will never get tired of telling.

My final purpose is to hopefully inspire the next generation of writers and filmmakers. This book will tell what has come before in the genre but it is up to you to decide what happens next. Find your own version and start telling someone about it. You are the future of vampire stories

Ghost Stories at the Villa Diodati:

The Birth of the Vampire

It was a dark and stormy night...

'He shut his eyes, hoping that it was but a vision arising from his disturbed imagination; but he again saw the same form, when he unclosed them, stretched by his side. There was no colour upon her cheek, not even upon her lip; yet there was a stillness about her face that seemed almost as attaching as the life that once dwelt there — upon her neck and breast was blood, and upon her throat were the marks of teeth having opened the vein — to this the men pointed, crying, simultaneously struck with horror, "Vampyre! a Vampyre!"'

— The Vampyre *by John Polidori*

ARY STOOD AT THE large window watching an electrical storm erupt over Geneva. Flashes of lightning lit up Lake Leman, which appeared to be boiling underneath the low, dark clouds. Every so often thunder would crack and boom, and in some distant room of the house Mary's younger step-sister, Claire, screamed.

It was June 1816, and nineteen-year-old Mary Wollstonecraft Godwin was staying in the Villa Diodati, a large mansion on the shores of the lake. The summer of 1816 is noted among meteorologists for its low temperatures and devastating storms. But it is also famous for something that happened one night in the house where Mary, Claire, and Mary's husband-to-be, the poet Percy Shelley, were

spending some time with the notorious Lord Byron
and his twenty-year-old personal physician, John
Polidori.

Byron, the clubfooted but otherwise devastatingly
handsome poet, was on the run. An affair with
his half-sister, Augusta, had scandalised London
society and destroyed his marriage. He was already
well-known for his affair with Lady Caroline Lamb,
who declared him 'mad, bad, and dangerous to
know'. He had escaped London pursued by would-
be biographers, moneylenders, and several women,
including Mary Shelley's step-sister, Claire, who
was pregnant with his child.

Mary and her husband were also on the run from
the scandal-mongering newspapers and drawing-
room whispers of London. Shelley had left his wife
for Mary, the young daughter of the philosopher
William Godwin. They had met at a dinner party
and fallen in love while picnicking on the grave
of Mary's mother, the early feminist writer, Mary
Wollstonecraft. Her father did not approve of the
match and Mary and Percy had been forced to leave
England. Claire tagged along as well, hoping to
meet up with Byron, the father of her unborn child.

Percy, Mary, and Claire arrived in Geneva in May 1816 and took up residence in the Hotel Angleterre. Byron arrived ten days later with Dr John Polidori. Percy Shelley and Byron had never met, but had read and admired each other's poetry. Claire introduced them on the shore of the lake and the pair hit it off immediately. The group began to socialise together at the hotel and to take boat trips on the lake. Unfortunately, the Angleterre was also filled with English tourists eager for a glimpse of Byron, the infamous noble, and his new friends. Guests in the hotel filled their letters with detailed reports of the young celebrities. No one knew exactly who belonged with who, and wild rumours trickled back to England. Byron and Polidori soon moved to a large house directly across the lake. The Villa Diodati was more private, but Byron missed the company of the others. He invited them to join him, not realising that he had set the stage for one of the most famous nights in literary history.

The gloomy weather kept the group indoors for most of the summer. After dinner, the residents of the house would assemble for a nightly round of ghost stories in front of a large open fire. While heavy rain fell outside, Byron, Mary, Percy, Claire and John took turns reading stories from a book called *Tales of the Dead*.

One night, Percy Shelley found himself growing increasingly nervous as he listened to another morbid tale in the candlelit room. When he could stand it no longer, he ran from the room screaming. The others followed him only to see him faint in the hallway. Polidori threw cold water on Percy's face to revive him. Percy, pale and shaking, told them that he had experienced a bizarre hallucination involving eyes that appeared all over Mary's body.

The creepy atmosphere created by the stories appealed to Byron and he decided that they should all have a go at writing a ghost story. Mary and John Polidori must have felt somewhat intimidated at the idea of competing with two of England's most famous poets. Ironically, it is their stories that are remembered today.

While trying to come up with an idea, Mary had a terrible nightmare that would inspire her story. She dreamt of a man on a table, built part by part by some kind of artist. Suddenly the man began to move. A voice screams, 'It's alive!'

Mary woke up, terrified but ready to write. Her story was about a young student who builds a man in laboratory but immediately regrets it. The creature pursues the student and eventually destroys him. Mary Shelley's contribution to the ghost story contest is one of the most influential novels of all time. It inspired countless other novels, plays, films, television shows, and plenty of nightmares. Some people say that it is the first science-fiction novel. She named the story after a castle that she and Percy had once visited. Mary's story was called *Frankenstein*.

There is no record that Percy Shelley ever wrote his ghost story. Perhaps he thought that his earlier performance had done enough to scare everyone. Byron, whose idea it was in the first place, grumpily announced that he could only write poems. He did mention something about a vampire story but never got around to actually writing anything more than a short fragment.

But John Polidori had fallen in love with Mary Shelley. He had considered challenging Percy to a duel but was discouraged by Byron who said that he would accept the challenge himself if it was issued. Byron also played a nasty trick on Polidori, or Polly Dolly, as he called him. Seeing Mary approaching the villa one afternoon, he somehow convinced Polidori that it would be a wonderful gesture to jump from a second-floor balcony and greet her. Polidori broke his ankle, and probably made a complete fool of himself. Now that a duel was out of the question and he could barely walk, he decided to write a ghost story, perhaps with a view to impressing Mary.

Unbeknownst to Byron and the other members of the group, Polidori was secretly keeping a journal of everything that happened in the house. Like a modern day paparazzi, he was being paid 500 pounds by a publisher, John Murray, who was planning to publish the journal. Byron was the subject of endless gossip and rumours. A tell-all insider account would have been nothing short of gold for an English editor in 1816. Throughout the summer, Polidori faithfully recorded, among other items, Byron's many affairs with women and his growing friendship with Percy Shelley.

Somehow, the journal and the idea for a ghost tale merged into the story of Lord Ruthven, an aristocratic vampire who resembled none other than Byron himself. The doctor couldn't have realised it at the time but he had just created one of the most enduring creatures in the popular imagination. His story was published a few years later as *The Vampyre*.

The First English Vampires

Until Polidori started writing, vampires were anything but suave. In the twelfth century, an English monk and historian named William of Newborough described a vampire-like creature as being 'swollen to an enormous corpulence' with blood. So instead of the smooth Count Dracula or handsome Edward, medieval villagers were faced with something resembling a giant leech.

In the Middle Ages, people believed that their bodies were simply vessels that contained a life-force or spirit. For medieval man, death was a matter of the spirit moving on to a new place, usually heaven or hell. The vessel of the body was buried in the ground but didn't necessarily remain there. Without the idea of a physical death, it was easy to imagine the body being occupied by another spirit and returning to terrorise the living. These stories were quite common in medieval Britain and represent the earliest English vampire stories.

The first reports were of possession. There is a famous story of a girl who went to pray one evening in her local church, unaware that the body of a recently deceased man had been placed near the altar. While she was praying, the body came to life. It was clear to her that she was dealing with the devil, so she picked up a large cross and bashed the living corpse until it lay down again. This unnamed girl may be the spiritual ancestor of Buffy and other vampire hunters. She was certainly not the last person to use a cross to defend herself against a vampire!

Later stories in medieval England were similar to ghost stories. Another writer from the twelfth century, Walter Map, tells a story about an evil man who died and was buried but started to return to his village at nightfall. When he reached the town he would call out the name of a particular neighbour. Within three days that neighbour would get sick and die. When the people of the village told the local bishop about the problem, he advised that they dig up the body and sprinkle it with holy water. The villagers tried this but the corpse kept returning. Eventually a knight called Sir William Laudun took the matter into his own hands. He waited until the corpse appeared and chased it back to its grave where he split the head in two with a heavy sword. This seemed to work where the holy water had failed.

Interestingly, when these stories were recorded, there was no discernible scepticism about their truth. Someone like Walter Map may have recorded a story of the living dead amid reports of failed crops or the visit of a noble. These chronicles were not collections of folk-tales or legends; they were histories. The writers seemed to believe these stories, and so presumably did the people whose lives were being chronicled. While vampire stories have become the domain of fantasy in our world, this wasn't always the case.

The Vampyre
by John Polidori

There was no way that bloated monsters covered in dirt were ever going to capture the imagination in any lasting way. John Polidori's story, *The Vampyre*, gave the creature a much-needed makeover in the guise of the handsome and utterly vicious Lord Ruthven.

Though Ruthven is the vampire, the main character of the story is a young gentleman called Aubrey, recently orphaned and responsible for his sister, Miss Aubrey. Aubrey has inherited a large fortune and has decided to travel to Europe. The 'grand tour' was a rite of passage for young gentlemen in Polidori's time. In fact, he and Byron were in the middle of an extended tour when he wrote the story. Aubrey learns that a certain Lord Ruthven, a charming but somewhat mysterious member of London high society, also has plans to go abroad. They meet and decide to go together.

Aubrey starts to notice that there is something strange about his travelling companion. At every stop, Ruthven seeks out a card game and plays for awhile, carefully observing the other players. Eventually he chooses a foolish young man and takes him for every cent. Instead of keeping the money, he then purposely loses it to another player. This seems unnecessarily cruel to Aubrey who wants to reason with his new friend but can never seem to find the right time to broach the subject.

When they reach Rome, Aubrey receives a letter from his guardians that warns him about Lord Ruthven. A woman whom the Lord has shamed has told the entire depraved story of their relationship. His guardians advise Aubrey to separate himself from Ruthven immediately. Aubrey finds that his friend has been courting a local woman. He sends a note to the woman's mother warning her about the Lord. He also tells Ruthven that he no longer wishes to travel with him.

Aubrey then visits Greece where he falls in love with a young Greek girl, Ianthe. The two are attacked by a vampire who kills the girl and seriously injures Aubrey, who lies close to death with a fever. Lord Ruthven reappears and looks after Aubrey until he is ready to travel again. When the

Lord is wounded in an attempted robbery, he makes Aubrey swear that he will never reveal what he knows of Ruthven. The Lord then dies and Aubrey returns to Rome where he finds that the woman courted by Ruthven has disappeared and her family has been ruined. He returns to England.

Back in England, Ruthven returns from the dead and Aubrey begins to lose his mind. While he is ill, Ruthven proposes to his sister, Miss Aubrey. Aubrey knows he is dying and on the night before the wedding, he writes a letter to his sister warning her about Ruthven. The letter is not delivered and Aubrey dies. On her wedding night, Miss Aubrey becomes the next victim. 'Aubrey's sister had glutted the thirst of a VAMPYRE!'

The story, though somewhat overwritten and melodramatic, is still entertaining. Lord Ruthven is an utterly compelling character who shares a number of traits with Lord Byron. Polidori cleverly uses Byron's reputation with women as the basis for the story. He simply goes one step further and creates a character that not only ruins a woman's reputation, but kills her too.

Aside from introducing two famous characters

into the popular imagination, the ghost story evening at the Villa Diodati seemed to have another effect. Within a few years, all of the men present there had died. Percy Shelley, an enthusiastic sailor but a very poor swimmer, drowned while sailing near Naples. Byron died of a fever while fighting for Greek independence. John Polidori, despite the success of his story, considered himself a great failure and committed suicide at the age of twenty-six. Was it just a strange coincidence — or the curse of the vampire?

THE MODERN VAMPIRE is a product of the late eighteenth century fashion for the Gothic novel. The Castle of Otranto *by Horace Walpole was first published in 1764 and is commonly considered the English starting point for this genre. Gothic literature was characterised by its use of medieval imagery, and settings such as old castles and abbeys. The stories were meant to frighten readers and usually involved themes of madness and evil. Monsters and supernatural creatures were also a feature. Gothic stories were popular throughout the nineteenth century and vampires were soon absorbed into this tradition. Gothic culture continues to thrive today in a number of manifestations including music, fashion, literature and film.*

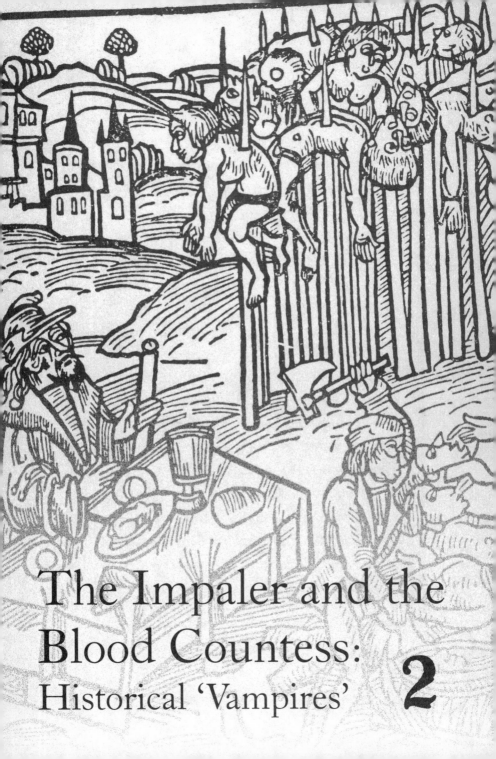

The Impaler and the Blood Countess:
Historical 'Vampires'

2

Obviously something happened...

'In all the darkest pages of the malign supernatural there is no more terrible tradition than that of the Vampire, a pariah even among demons. Foul are his ravages; gruesome and seemingly barbaric are the ancient and approved methods by which folk must rid themselves of this hideous pest. Even today in certain quarters of the world, in remoter districts of Europe itself, Transylvania, Slavonia, the isles and mountains of Greece, the peasant will take the law into his own hands and utterly destroy the carrion who — as it is yet firmly believed — at night will issue from his unhallowed grave to spread the infection of vampirism throughout the countryside.'

— The Vampire *by Montague Summers*

THERE IS ONE HISTORICAL figure that will forever be associated with vampires. His name was Vlad III, or, as he is better known, Vlad the Impaler. In the fifteenth century he was the ruler of Wallachia, a medieval nation, which is today part of Romania. He successfully defended his small nation against the superpowers of the day and remains a hero to many people for his bravery and steadfast belief in the sovereignty of his small country.

So how did he become associated with vampires?

Vlad lived in dangerous times and his country was a battleground. It was caught between two empires. The Ottoman Turks were on one side and the Hungarian Empire was on the other. A leader of Wallachia had to be either very smart or simply terrifying. Vlad the Impaler chose the latter.

Unlike England and France, a prince of Wallachia did not automatically assume the throne upon the death of his father. Instead, there was a complicated system that involved a type of election by the other nobles. Usually, this meant that the most powerful noble became leader, or *Voivod*, after murdering his predecessor and all of his followers. Taking the throne of Wallachia was not for the meek!

Vlad the Impaler was born in 1431 in Transylvania, a neighbouring province of Hungary (today part of Romania). When he was five, his father returned to Wallachia, murdered the reigning ruler, and became the Voivod. His father was also named Vlad, and became Vlad II when he took the throne. Vlad II belonged to a special group of Christian knights, known as the Order of the Dragon. In Romanian, the word for dragon is *drac*, and the definite article, or 'the', is *ul*. Therefore Vlad's father was Vlad Dracul.

Ula means 'the son of', so the young Vlad was known as Dracula, or 'son of the dragon'. In Romanian, however, drac also means 'devil'.

Vlad II spent his reign trying to keep both the Ottoman and Hungarian empires from occupying Wallachia. In return for Ottoman support, he sent his 12-year-old son, Vlad Dracula, to the Sultan as a hostage. Vlad spent six years in a place called Adrianople (which is now the city of Edirne in western Turkey). Presumably the young Wallachian had plenty of time to consider his own future career.

In 1447 Vlad II was captured and buried alive by the Hungarians. Sixteen-year-old Vlad Dracula, supported by the Turks, made his move and successfully captured the throne of Wallachia. He lasted two months before being ousted by a distant cousin. He went into exile in Transylvania and remained there until 1456 when, with the help of the Hungarians this time, he was able to take back his country. He built a castle in the mountains and began a reign of terror over his people.

It was during this time that Vlad Dracula became Vlad Tepes. The word *tepes* means 'impaler,' as Vlad Dracula liked to impale his enemies on large stakes or poles. He started with the people who had collaborated in his father's death but quickly moved on to just about anyone else who crossed his path. It was an unpleasant way to die. The victims expired slowly on their stakes and were left rotting in the fields as a warning to others. In 1461, the Turkish army retreated after coming across 20 000 staked corpses outside of a town called Turgoviste. Vlad seemed to enjoy the spectacle of people on stakes and often arranged them in geometrical shapes.

Even by the standards of the time, Vlad was a figure of evil. After he became Voivod, he noticed that there were a lot of beggars in Wallachia. He issued an invitation to all of them for a great feast to be held in the capital. At the end of the night, he asked if they would like to be free of all of their burdens. When they all cried, 'yes', Vlad ordered that the doors of the hall be secured. He then burned it to the ground, killing everyone inside.

He is also famous for taking great offence when a group of foreign dignitaries neglected to remove their hats in his presence. Vlad ordered that the hats be nailed to their heads so that they would have an excuse for their rudeness.

But his most notorious moment came in 1459 after he had 30 000 people put to the stake in the city of Brasov. So that his nobles could appreciate the work of their ruler, he ordered that a great feast be held among the corpses. During the feast, any noble who was seen to be turned off his food by the terrible stench of rotting bodies soon found himself on a stake. Far from finding the atmosphere unpleasant for dining himself, Vlad terrified his subjects by drinking the blood of his victims.

By the time he was overthrown by his brother in 1462, he had murdered most of the nobles of his own country, as well as countless soldiers, diplomats and travellers from abroad. His wife committed suicide by jumping from the walls of his mountain castle, and his other relatives lived in terror that he would have them put to the stake. When he was deposed, he escaped into Hungary where he was immediately arrested and imprisoned. He is rumoured to have spent his time in prison capturing mice and birds to impale on tiny stakes.

In 1476 he successfully invaded Wallachia again, this time assisted by a Transylvanian prince named Stephen Bathory. He returned to the throne, but

only for a short time. The Turks invaded and Vlad
was killed in battle. He was so notorious that his
head was sent to Constantinople so that it could
be displayed as proof that he was truly dead. Not
surprisingly, it was placed on a stake. The rest
of him was buried in Bucharest, the modern day
capital of Romania.

The Lady was a Vampire

But it may have been a woman who was the
real model for the nineteenth-century vampire.
Elizabeth Bathory was a blood-obsessed serial-killer
and a member of the Hungarian nobility. Vlad the
Impaler, in a court of law, might have claimed that
he was just trying to protect his country from its
enemies. Bathory had no such excuse.

There is an interesting connection between
Elizabeth and Vlad the Impaler. The Bathory
family was a large and powerful clan that included
kings and nobles all over Eastern Europe. When
Vlad attempted to regain control of Wallachia in
1476, it was Elizabeth's ancestor, Stephen Bathory,

that he called upon for assistance.

Elizabeth Bathory was born in 1560 to a noble Hungarian family. When she was fifteen, she was married off to Ferenc Nadasy, another Hungarian noble. Ferenc had a taste for battle and was rarely home on the large estate where they lived. It was during his absences that the trouble began.

Servants were treated harshly by their employers at this time, but Elizabeth seemed to take special pleasure in punishing the female servants. There are reports that she would sometimes pour cold water on them and leave them outside to freeze while watching from the window.

Then she made a strange discovery. One night, while beating a young servant girl, Bathory noticed that the blood that covered her hands seemed to be making her skin look less old and wrinkled. She began to bathe in the blood of young women, and her demand for blood slowly increased. She combed the countryside for victims, offering them employment in her household.

The disappearance and death of servant girls could be ignored, but Bathory made a grave error when she began murdering young noble women.

When certain noble families began to complain, the King of Hungary had to take action. In 1610, Elizabeth Bathory was arrested in her castle. According to eyewitness accounts, the castle was filled with imprisoned young women who had been abducted and tortured.

She never stood trial; the Bathory family simply refused to allow the trial to take place. Instead, she was walled up in a room in her castle and fed through a tiny slit in the brickwork. She died in 1614 and had to be buried far away from her home as the villagers near the castle refused to allow her to be placed in the local churchyard.

Elizabeth Bathory and Vlad the Impaler were bad news. Their crimes are well-documented and there is no doubt that they are exceptional figures of horror. But were they vampires? There is no evidence that either possessed extraordinary powers and both appear to have been quite mortal. Vlad the Impaler was the inspiration for Bram Stoker's *Dracula* who, in turn, inspired countless other stories. Bathory is less well-known but has certainly become an important model for writers and filmmakers attempting to create a female vampire.

Buffy's Ancestors: Hunting Vampires in the Age of Reason

The Enlightenment, or the Age of Reason, is the period that saw people farewelling superstition and folk-tales for science and rational explanations. It was a time for mathematics and careful observations. And vampires. For some reason, along with the discovery of the laws of gravity, the eighteenth century featured a growing fear of vampires that resulted in widespread hysteria and the birth of the vampire hunter.

In 1732, a report was made to the authorities in Belgrade (the capital of modern-day Serbia) that a vampire was terrorising a family in a remote village. A group of soldiers, lawyers, doctors and a prince, visited the village to investigate. They were told that the vampire was a man who had died and been buried in the village three years earlier. In a two-week period, he rose from the grave and murdered four members of his own family by sucking their blood. He was caught drinking from his niece's throat and chased away.

When night fell, the group made their way to the local graveyard and dug up the man's body. They were surprised to find that he had not decayed in the slightest and was lying with his eyes wide open. According to some reports, the heart was still beating. The head was cut off and a stake was driven through the heart. Then they filled the coffin with heavy rocks and reburied it. The vampire left the family alone and the group returned to Belgrade.

However the most famous eighteenth century case involved a soldier called Arnold Paole. Paole was killed one afternoon in 1725, when a cart on which he was riding flipped over and landed on top of him. A month after he was buried, it was reported that he rose from the grave and killed four people, before returning to his grave. The report claims he killed them in a manner in keeping with the 'habits of a vampire'. Then one of his fellow soldiers remembered that Paole had told him a frightening story about an experience that took place when he was fighting in Turkey. According to Paole, he had been attacked by a vampire and badly wounded. He had tried to cure himself by eating earth from the vampire's grave, but to no avail. When his body was exhumed, it was reported as being flushed and healthy-looking. Once again, the eyes were wide open. Paole's head was cut off, a stake was driven through his heart, and this time the body was burnt. But the damage had already been done, and the vampire attacks continued in the village. His four victims were dug up and given the same treatment. This slowed the vampire activity but did not stop it. The vampire Paole had been attacking animals as well as people, and those who had eaten the animals and died were now also vampires. By the time the villagers felt safe again, virtually all of the recent dead in the cemetery had been dug up, beheaded, stabbed with stakes, and burnt.

These scenes were repeated all over Eastern Europe until finally the Empress of Austria, the enlightened Maria Theresa, outlawed the practice of digging up graves and declared that vampirism was a myth. She later outlawed the burning of witches as well.

Many of the vampire stories from this period were reported by a Benedictine monk called Dom

Augustine Calmet. Calmet did not necessarily believe that vampires existed, but he certainly did not dismiss the idea completely. Plenty of his material was based on first-hand accounts, often by credible sources. 'This is a mysterious and difficult matter,' said Calmet. 'I leave bolder and more proficient minds to resolve it.'

One bolder mind was that of Jean Jaques Rousseau, the leading philosopher of the time, who wrote: 'If ever there was in the world a warranted and proven history, it is that of vampires.' He seemed to believe that there was enough evidence of the existence of vampires that they couldn't be completely dismissed as fiction. Two hundred years later, in the 1970s, a well-known writer called Colin Wilson said of eighteenth century accounts of vampires, 'Obviously something happened, and it seems unlikely that it was pure imagination.'

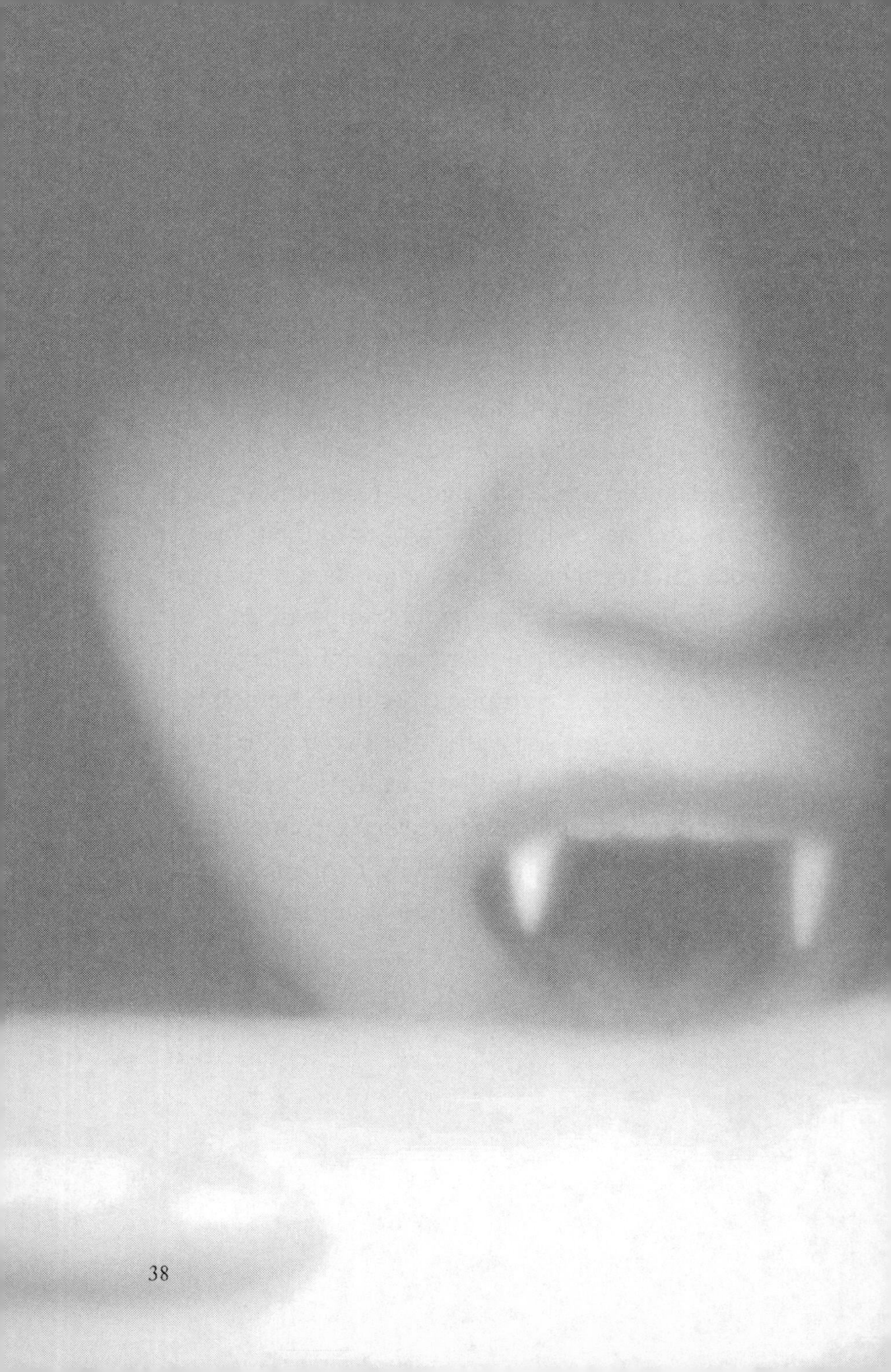

*U*NTIL RECENTLY, THE *vampire was closely associated with Greece. In Greek mythology, a character called Lamia inspired a class of demons called the Lamiai who drank blood. Later, tales of the vrykolakas were widespread in Greece. These creatures were revenants who had escaped from their graves and roamed the earth. Less than 40 years ago, visitors to remote villages in Greece were still being told stories about encounters with the vrykolakas. When Polidori wrote the first modern vampire story in the early nineteenth century, he set an important scene in Greece. Transylvania has become the place most closely associated with the creature, but that was largely due to Bram Stoker. Before* Dracula, *Greece was the land of the vampire.*

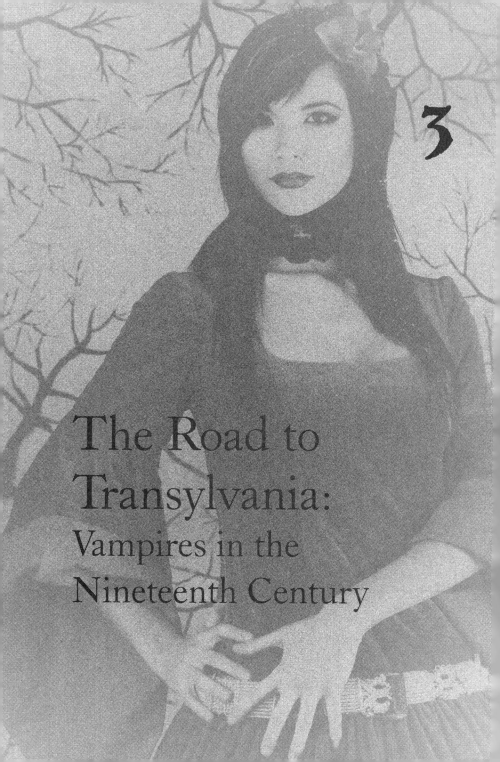

The Road to Transylvania:
Vampires in the Nineteenth Century

3

The girl has swooned...

'I mean, to decapitate the monster,' he answered, with a fierce flush and a stamp that echoed mournfully through the hollow ruin, and his clenched hand was at the same moment raised, as if it grasped the handle of an axe, while he shook it ferociously in the air.

'What?' exclaimed my father, more than ever bewildered.

'To strike her head off.'

'Cut her head off!'

'Aye, with a hatchet, with a spade, or with anything that can cleave through her murderous throat. You shall hear,' he answered, trembling with rage.

— Carmilla *by Sheridan Le Fanu*

L ORD RUTHVEN MAY HAVE been the first
notable English vampire, but another figure
looms even larger. Until the appearance
of Count Dracula in the 1890s, the most famous
vampire in England was a man named Varney.
Varney the Vampire was the creation of a Scottish
writer named James Malcolm Rhymer. The story
appeared in a series of short books that were known
as 'penny dreadfuls'.

In the nineteenth century, the principal source
of entertainment for most people came in printed
stories that appeared on a weekly basis in a small
booklet or pamphlet. The cover was usually

a sensational picture depicting a scene from the story. Readers would eagerly await the next part of the story in the same manner that people today wait for the next episode of a their favourite television show. The name 'penny dreadful' referred firstly to the price. More established writers like Charles Dickens published their stories in short chapters that usually cost one shilling or twelve pennies. The penny dreadfuls were aimed at teenage readers but were read by all kinds of people. 'Dreadful' might have referred to the writing. The stories were filled with exciting and bloody scenes, and there was lots of action, but the plots often made little sense. Depending on demand, characters might die suddenly in one edition and be brought back to life in the next. Sometimes a character would be evil one week and good the next. However, they were very popular, and stories like *Sweeney Todd* first appeared in this form. *Varney the Vampire* may be the most influential of the penny dreadfuls.

The first chapter of Rhymer's story appeared in 1845 and the series ran until 1847. It was a penny dreadful, but appealed to a much wider audience. Vampires were quite a feature of popular culture at this time. Karl Marx, the father of communism, was writing his masterwork, *Das Kapital*, and regularly used vampire metaphors. The theatres were filled with adaptations of Polidori's story and other stories of the undead. Queen Victoria's diaries from this time record a visit to the theatre to watch a vampire play. 'Very trashy,' was the monarch's verdict.

When *Varney the Vampire* was finally published in its complete form, it was nearly 1000 pages long and divided into 220 chapters. It is a challenging read though some of the individual scenes are very frightening even today. The first chapter introduces a famous tradition in vampire stories — that of the creature attacking his female victim as she sleeps in her bedroom. There is an electrical storm raging outside and the beautiful young woman is woken up by the thunder. Lightning flashes and she catches a glimpse of something outside:

'What was it?' she gasped, 'real or delusion? A figure tall and gaunt, endeavouring from the outside to unclasp the window, I saw it. That flash of lightning revealed it to me.'

She lies staring at the window for a minute or two, too scared to even scream. The vampire, in the manner of a petty thief, breaks a pane of glass and reaches in to lift the latch. Now the figure is coming towards her and she can see it clearly:

It (the face) is perfectly white — perfectly bloodless. The eyes look like polished tin; the lips are drawn back, and the principal feature next to those dreadful eyes is the teeth — the fearful looking teeth — projecting like those of some wild animal, hideously, glaringly white, and fang-like.

The vampire approaches the bed, grabs her by the hair and:

With a plunge he seizes her neck in his fang-like teeth — a gush of blood, and a hideous sucking noise follows. The girl has swooned and the vampire is at his hideous repast!

So ends the first instalment of *Varney the Vampire*, with another 219 to come. It would be another week before readers would find out what

happened next. Though largely forgotten today,
Varney made several important contributions to
vampire lore. This is the first time that the fangs are
mentioned as part of the creature's appearance. It is
also the first time that those fangs are used to make
two distinctive punctures on the neck. Varney, like
Dracula and the many vampires that followed, has
the strength of a superhero and can hypnotise his
victims. Varney is also the first vampire that elicits
a kind of sympathy from the reader. Until this
point, vampires had been characters of pure evil.
Varney eventually tells the sad story of how he
got into such a state and how much he much
he despises himself. This approach to telling a
vampire story reappears most significantly in the
1970s, when the novelist Anne Rice created the
sensitive undead soul, Louis, in *Interview with the
Vampire*. There might even be something of Varney
in Stephenie Meyer's Edward.

Varney's story is a long one. After the first
instalment, the plot meanders around as Varney
terrorises, then befriends a particular family. He
has countless adventures, but in the end he has
renounced evil and is determined to destroy himself

by jumping into the crater of the volcano of Mt Vesuvius. A guide accompanies him to the edge of the crater and is told:

'You will say that you accompanied Varney the Vampire to the crater of Mt Vesuvius, and that, tired and disgusted with a life of horror, he flung himself in to prevent the possibility of a reanimation of his remains.'

Before the guide could utter anything but a shriek, Varney took one tremendous leap, and disappeared into the burning mouth of the mountain.

Goodbye Varney but hello to a new kind of vampire story. From now on the vampire will be less monster and more human, while still retaining the ability to terrify. The vampire was no longer to be confused with zombies escaping from the grave or mischievous poltergeists. It was now a unique character whose popularity would continue to rise throughout the nineteenth century.

Carmilla

Sheridan Le Fanu is considered the finest ghost-
story writer of the nineteenth century. The Irish
journalist began writing his spooky tales while still
in university. His stories are very subtle. He does
not try to shock his readers with blood-soaked
scenes of horror, but instead quietly suggests that
something extremely creepy is occurring. His
ghost stories remain frightening and are well worth
seeking out, but he is also famous for producing
a vampire novella that would define the female
vampire in virtually all films and books to come.
The eerie Carmilla was not the first female vampire.
Wake Not the Dead, sometimes attributed the
German writer Johann Ludwig Tieck, predates
Polidori's story and features a female vampire
named Brunhilde. The English Romantic poet
Samuel Taylor Coleridge's poem *Christabel* features
an other-worldly woman called Geraldine who
haunts the title character and her father. Towards
the end of *Varney the Vampire*, Varney turns
a woman called Clara Crofton into a vampire. But

it was Le Fanu's creature that caught the popular imagination.

Carmilla begins with a short prologue that tells the reader that the story they are about to read is by a correspondent who has since died. The storyteller turns out to be a young woman named Laura who lives with her father in a remote castle in a country in Eastern Europe called Styria. She starts by describing an experience that she had when she was six years old. She reports that she was alone in her bedroom — always dangerous in vampire stories — when a beautiful young woman appeared to her:

I looked at her with a kind of pleased wonder and ceased whimpering. She caressed me with her hands and lay down beside me on the bed and drew me towards her, smiling; I felt immediately delightfully soothed, and fell asleep again. I was wakened by a sensation as if two needles ran into my breast very deep at the same moment, and I cried loudly.

The story then jumps ahead twelve years when Laura is eighteen. A neighbour, General Spielsdorf, writes to inform Laura and her father that his daughter has died of a mysterious illness. Feeling melancholy about the news, Laura and her father take an evening stroll. They witness a carriage accident and rush to help. A young woman has been knocked unconscious and it is clear that she cannot travel. Laura's father assures the girl's mother that they will take good care of her and she is carried to the castle where a doctor is summoned.

Laura is curious about the visitor, who appears to be about her age. When the girl, Carmilla, recovers, the two grow close. Carmilla is vague about her life and only admits that she comes from an ancient family. Laura would like to know more about her new friend and is slightly mystified by Carmilla's ardour towards her. The mysterious girl tells her:

'You are mine, you shall be mine, you and I are one forever.'

Laura does not know what to make of this but is even more surprised at Carmilla's reaction to a hymn being sung by a passing funeral party. The funeral is for the young daughter of a local man, one of several young women who have died mysteriously in recent days. Carmilla has some kind of fit and blames it on the hymn.

Later in the story, a painting is delivered to the castle. It is a portrait of a woman called Mircalla, Countess Karnstein, and it is dated 1698. The woman in the picture looks exactly like Carmilla. The Karnsteins, once a noble family in the area, are all buried in a chapel nearby

Not long afterwards, Laura has another frightening dream about a demon that comes into her bedroom while she is sleeping:

'But I soon saw that it was a sooty black animal that resembled a monstrous cat. It appeared to me about four or five feet long for it measured fully the length of the hearthrug as it passed over it; and it continued to-ing and fro-ing with the lithe sinister restlessness of a beast in a cage.'

Once again she feels the two sharp stinging pains in her chest and cries out. Soon after, Laura becomes ill and her father summons the doctor who orders that she not be left alone.

Eventually General Spielsdorf comes to visit with

the sad tale of his daughter's death. Months before, he had met a woman, a Countess, at a masked ball who told him that her daughter, Millarca, had suffered an accident in a fall from a horse and was still recovering. The Countess had to make an important journey and wondered if the General could look after the girl. He agreed, thinking that the girl would make a charming companion for his daughter. But soon his daughter became ill and died, complaining that two needles were piercing her chest.

The General is told by a local woodsman that vampires have been seen near the Karnstein chapel. They realise something about the names of the two visitors has something in common with the woman in the painting:

Carmilla
Mircalla
Millarca

Figured it out yet? The names are anagrams of each other, meaning that they contain the same letters in different orders. Laura's father and the

General alert the authorities and the coffin of Mircalla Karnstein is opened:

The features, though a hundred and fifty years had passed since her funeral, were tinted with the warmth of life. Her eyes were open; no cadaverous smell exhaled from the coffin.

When they discover a light heartbeat, they realise that there is only one course of action available:

Here then, were all the admitted signs of and proofs of vampirism. The body, therefore, in accordance with the ancient practice, was raised and a sharp stake was driven through the heart of the vampire, who uttered a piercing shriek... Then the head was struck off, and a torrent of blood flowed from the severed neck. The body and head was next placed on a pile of wood, and reduced to ashes, which were thrown upon the river and borne away, and that territory has never since been plagued by the visits of a vampire.

At the end of the story, Laura tells the reader that she still sometimes thinks that she hears Carmilla's light steps at the drawing room door. We know from the prologue that she has died soon after and the story ends with a delicious ambiguity about whether or not the vampire has actually been destroyed.

Except for Bram Stoker's *Dracula*, no vampire story has inspired more film versions than Sheridan Le Fanu's *Carmilla*. The spectacle of a beautiful young female vampire has been hard for horror directors to resist. But it is also a good story. Laura's mixed feelings about Carmilla are echoed by Stephenie Meyer's Bella when confronted with Edward. The combination of danger and charm sets the vampire apart from monsters like the werewolf. The drama in vampire stories is not so much about escaping from the vampire as deciding how one feels about the creature.

Sheridan Le Fanu employed several of the innovations introduced in *Varney the Vampire*. Carmilla has razor sharp teeth and uses them to leave small holes in her victims. She also possesses superhuman strength and the ability to appear in the form of animals. One innovation made in

Carmilla is the anagrammatic name changes, the idea that vampires can only disguise their original identity by shuffling the order of the letters in their name. Subsequent writers of vampire stories have toyed with this — Alucard and Dr Alcula have turned up in stories — but otherwise this has never really become a real feature of vampire lore. Nevertheless, when the most important of all vampires, Count Dracula, appeared 25 years later, the influence of *Carmilla* was undeniable.

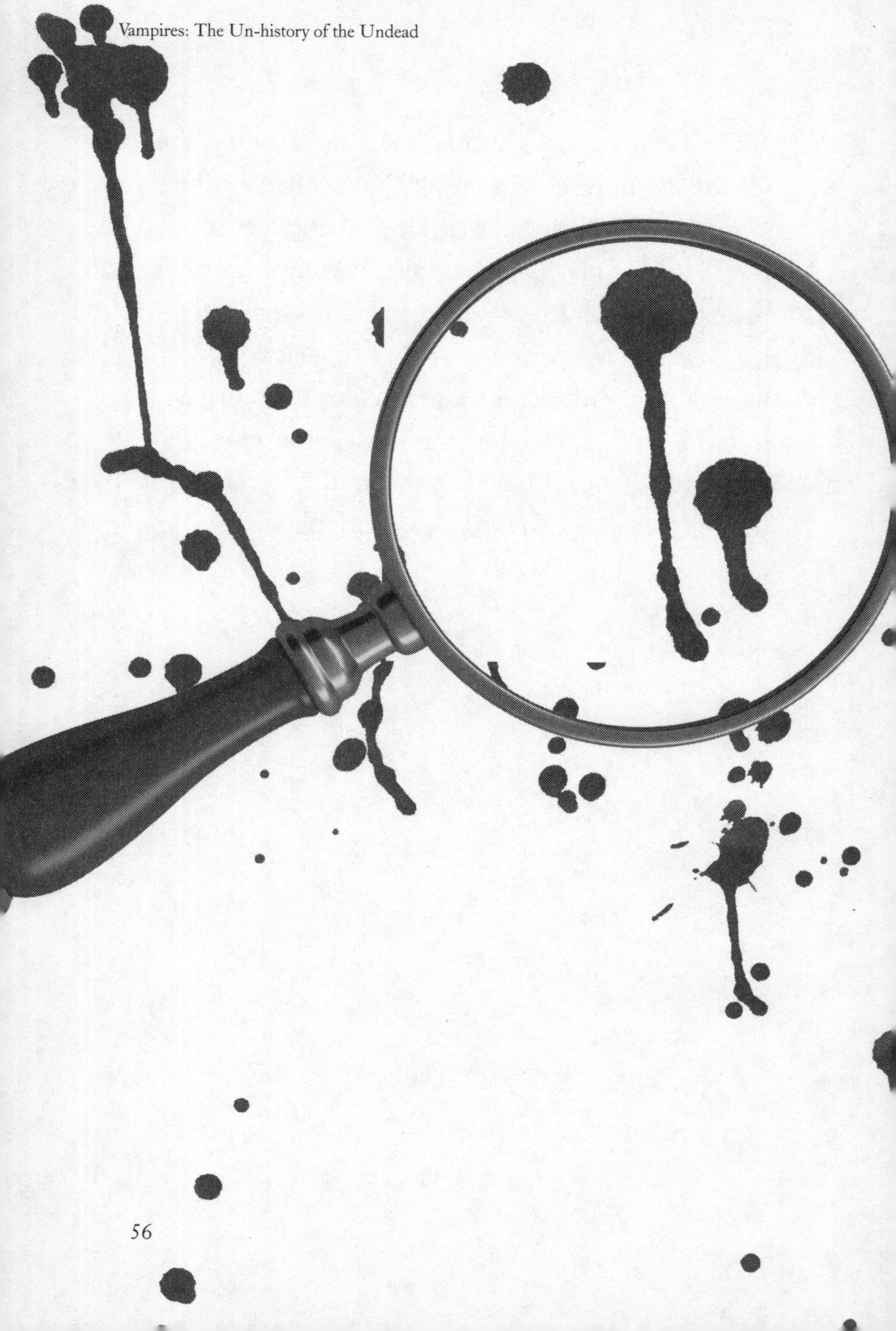

*S*INCE *ARTHUR CONAN DOYLE'S
*Sherlock Holmes was created during
the period in which Count Dracula
made his first appearance in fiction, it would
make sense that the famous detective would
sooner or later be faced with a vampire.* The
Adventure of the Sussex Vampire *is one of
the original 56 Holmes short stories.*

*A man believes that his Peruvian wife is
a vampire and that she has been sucking the
blood out of their newborn infant. As usual,
Holmes discovers that nothing so fanciful as
a vampire is involved and that there is
a rational, if somewhat bizarre,
explanation. You will have to read the story
if you want to know how it ends. It appears
in* The Casebook of Sherlock Holmes *by
Arthur Conan Doyle.*

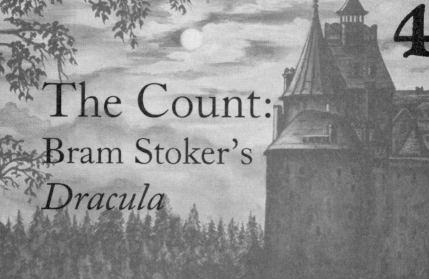

The Count:
Bram Stoker's
Dracula

Jonathan

Listen to them — the children of the night. What music they make!

'There was one great tomb more lordly than all the rest; huge it was, and nobly proportioned. On it was but one word:

DRACULA

This then was the Un-Dead home of the King Vampire, to whom so many more were due. Its emptiness spoke eloquent to make certain what I knew.'

— Dracula, *by Bram Stoker*

BRAM STOKER'S 1897 NOVEL, *Dracula*, introduced a vampire who has become one of the most famous fictional characters in history. With the possible exception of Sherlock Holmes, no literary figure has inspired more films than the Transylvanian Count. There have been more than 160 movies with a character called Dracula since the 1930s. That equates to one film every six months for the past 80 years, and means that since well before the Second World War, there has always been a Dracula movie playing somewhere. And that is in addition to countless retellings in novels, comic books, television shows, and songs. Not bad for a writer whose other books have all but disappeared and who died nearly penniless.

Dracula is a frightening novel and the vampire that Stoker created is a very unpleasant figure. He is the embodiment of evil and at no point in the story does the reader feel anything but sheer terror when he appears. Unlike Polidori's Lord Ruthven who seems to be able to move quite easily among human beings, Dracula has only one objective, and that is to drink the blood of his victims. There is none of Varney's regret and pain about the Count. Unlike Carmilla, he doesn't bother trying to make friends first before sinking his sharp teeth into someone's neck. This vampire is a serial-killer. Stoker's novel appeared less than ten years after the serial-killer Jack the Ripper terrified London with his grisly murders. The case has never been solved but there is evidence that Bram Stoker knew at least one of the many suspects. Vampires generally reflect the age in which they are created, and Dracula is no exception. A sinister figure preying on women would have appealed to an audience of readers who had been electrified by the sensational stories surrounding the Ripper murders.

The novel is told through a series of diary entries and letters by various characters. The idea was to present the book as a sort of dossier. This had been employed successfully by other writers and was intended to suggest the findings of an investigation. The first section of the novel is narrated by a young solicitor called Jonathan Harker who has been dispatched from London to close a real-estate deal with a mysterious nobleman who lives in a castle in Eastern Europe. Stoker was the first writer to connect Vlad the Impaler to the vampire story. The idea of using Eastern European nobles began with *Carmilla* and in an early draft of *Dracula*, Stoker used similar placenames. It is clear that Le Fanu's novella was an important influence. Female vampires make an early appearance in the story. Jonathan Harker's reaction to them follows Carmilla and sets the stage for the long series of alluring female vampires that have dominated films and books:

'The fair girl…bent over me, fairly gloating. There was a deliberate voluptuousness which was both thrilling and repulsive, and as she arched her neck she actually licked her lips like an animal, till I could see in the moonlight the moisture shining on

the scarlet lips and on the red tongue as it lapped the white sharp teeth.'

Harker somehow manages to survive this encounter and eventually escapes from the castle. Meanwhile back in England, his fiancée, Mina Murray, is corresponding with a friend, Lucy Westenra. When Lucy begins sleepwalking and looking increasingly pale, it becomes clear that the Count has arrived in England. With the tell-tale holes in her neck and her teeth looking sharper all the time, she slowly succumbs to the Count. Her fiancé consults with another of Lucy's suitors, Dr Seward, who in turn contacts his old teacher, Dr Abraham Van Helsing. When the older physician sees Lucy he recognises the symptoms immediately. He tries a series of blood transfusions but cannot save her. After her death and burial in a London cemetery, local children begin to disappear. Other children talk about the 'bloofer' (beautiful) lady who lives in the cemetery. Van Helsing pursues the young vampire into her tomb where a stake is driven through her heart. He also cuts off her head and fills it with garlic cloves.

Jonathan Harker eventually recovers from his ordeal in Dracula's castle and returns to England, now married to Lucy's friend Mina. When Van Helsing reads Harker's diary, he realises that there is a very powerful vampire on the loose in England who must be stopped. Along with Dr Seward, an American called Quincy Morris, and Lucy's former fiancé Arther Holmwood, Van Helsing begins to actively pursue the vampire with the help of the Harkers. Part of the investigation involves an inmate at the lunatic asylum where Dr Seward works. A man called Renfield has been eating bugs and raving about the 'master'.

Van Helsing and the team manage to track down the boxes of Transylvanian earth that the Count has shipped to England and 'purify' most of them with holy water. Unfortunately, the Count has begun to prey on Mina, who is slowly slipping into a vampiric state. There is no time lose if she is to be saved. As they close in on Dracula, he escapes back to his own country. They catch up with him in the mountains in the shadow of his castle. It is dusk and he is being carried by gypsies who attempt to stop the team from murdering him.

Mina's journal records his death:

*'I saw the Count lying within the box upon the
earth, some of which the rude falling of the cart had
scattered over him. He was deathly pale, just like
a waxen image, and the red eyes glared with the
horrible vindictive look which I knew too well...*

*But, on the instant, came the sweep and flash of
Jonathan's great knife. I shrieked as I saw it shear
through the throat; whilst at the same moment Mr
Morris's bowie knife plunged into the heart.*

*It was like a miracle; but before our very eyes and
almost in the drawing of a breath, the whole body
crumbled into dust and passed from our sight.'*

The novel introduced several important elements
to the vampire story. The association with bats
probably began with some of the illustrations in
Varney the Vampire, but Stoker established the
possibility of the vampire changing into a bat when
necessary. He was probably aware of the existence
of the vampire bat, a creature that, unlike the more
common fruit bat, feeds on the blood of other
creatures. There are three species of vampire bats

and they are found in Central and South America. The most common, *Desmodus rotundus*, has sharp teeth and an anticoagulant in their saliva that keeps the blood of their prey flowing while they lap it up, kitten-style. Quincey Morris mentions these bats in the novel. Not long before Stoker began *Dracula*, Charles Darwin published the first scientific account of the strange creatures. Generally, they do not attack humans though there are several accounts of people waking up to find a bat feasting on them.

Dracula also presented the crucifix as a weapon against vampires. This too has remained an important part of vampire lore. Stoker introduced the idea that the vampire was more than simply undead, but was also in league with the devil. This idea has also been explored in many films and books.

Stoker's other innovations include the lack of a reflection in a mirror, the ability to turn into mist, and the famously sharp fangs. He also introduced the idea that daylight robbed vampires of their power, although the idea that it was deadly to them appears only in a later film version of the book.

The Master

Dracula's author, Bram Stoker, is almost as
mysterious as his famous creation. He was born
in Ireland in 1847, and like so many other writers,
spent a great deal of his childhood in bed beset
by various illnesses. He recovered his health and
went on to steal Oscar Wilde's girlfriend, Florence
Balcomb, and marry her in 1878. Soon after, the
couple moved to London where Stoker became
involved in the vibrant London theatre scene.

The most famous actor of the day was a man
named Henry Irving. He is best remembered for
his electrifying performances in various Shakespeare
plays. Upon arriving in London, Bram Stoker
became fascinated by Irving and began to attend all
of his shows. One night Stoker was so overcome by
Irving's performance that he suffered some kind of
hysterical fit. He devoted the rest of his life to the
actor, becoming his personal assistant and managing
the Lyceum Theatre, which Irving owned. Stoker's
only child was named Irving Noel Stoker. It was
a strange and obsessive relationship. Irving was
known for his portrayal of villains like Shakespeare's

Richard III. Many people have speculated that he may have been the model for Count Dracula. Bram Stoker may have cast himself in the role of Jonathan Harker, a man who inadvertently ends up under the spell of the powerful vampire. Stoker, apparently, hoped that his hero, Irving, would play the role on stage. However Irving was not impressed by his disciple's novel, and pronounced it 'dreadful'.

Most of the reviews at the time were positive. The *Daily Mail* called it, 'a weird, powerful and horrible story'. Some reviewers thought, perhaps justifiably, that it was too long and dragged at points. The most glowing praise came from Stoker's mother who said that it was better than *Frankenstein* and would guarantee his place in literary history. Most readers regarded it as an adventure story with a supernatural theme, rather than as the iconic Gothic story that is has become for today's readers.

It didn't sell well at the time and probably would have disappeared like so many other novels, had it not been for the popular theatrical production that followed. Stoker himself died in 1912 without seeing any evidence that he had produced one of the most important horror novels of all time. His wife sold the theatrical copyright to an actor and director named Hamilton Deane who adapted the story himself and put it on the stage in 1924.

Deane's production is an important part of the vampire story. Stoker's Dracula is not a charming character. He is a noble but is described as having a large white moustache, pointy ears, and bushy eyebrows. The Count is a sly and dangerous figure but lacks the charm of Polidori's Lord Ruthven. Hamilton Deane recast Dracula as a suave killer. To emphasize his charms, he put Dracula in the waistcoat and cape that have become almost synonymous with this character. The moustache, bushy eyebrows and pointy ears were dropped as well.

Hamilton Deane had intended to play the part of Dracula himself. He had thrilled audiences playing Frankenstein for many years and was on the look-out for a new monster. Eventually he decided to take the Van Helsing role. The play premiered in Derby, England, and the role of Dracula was taken by Raymond Huntley, an actor who continued to appear in movies and television shows well into the 1970s. The play toured England for three years and was a huge success. Audiences found it terrifying and all of the ushers were given smelling salts so that they could revive patrons who fainted during the performance. In 1927, the play opened in New York with a revised script and a new cast. Again it was a hit. This time though, Dracula was played by a man who came from a tiny village near Transylvania. His name was Bela Lugosi, and no one, not even Bram Stoker, has become more closely associated with Count Dracula.

*H*UNDREDS, IF NOT THOUSANDS *of books involving Dracula have appeared since Bram Stoker's original was published in 1897. However, it was only in 2008 that the first official sequel was released. It was co-written by Bram's great-grand nephew, Dacre Stoker, a former Olympic pentathlon coach, and vampire expert, Ian Holt. The book is called* Dracula: The Un Dead *which was the original title of Stoker's book. Like its predecessor, it is written as a series of letters and involves many of the same characters. It is set in 1912, approximately 25 years after* Dracula *ends, and Bram Stoker himself appears in the story. A film is rumoured to be in the works. It will be the first version approved by the Stoker family since the 1931 movie starring Bela Lugosi.*

5

Bela Lugosi is Dead:

Vampire Films Part One

I never drink…wine…

Count Dracula: 'Van Helsing. Now that you have learned what you have learned, it would be well for you to return to your own country.'

Van Helsing: 'I prefer to remain and protect those whom you would destroy.'

Count Dracula: 'You are too late. My blood now flows through her veins. She will live through the centuries to come, as I have lived.'

Van Helsing: 'Should you escape us, Dracula, we know how to save Miss Mina's soul if not her life.'

Count Dracula: 'If she dies by day. But I shall see that she dies by night.'

Van Helsing: 'And I will have Carfax Abbey torn down, stone by stone, excavated a mile around. I will find your earth-box and drive that stake through your heart.'

— Dracula, *directed by Tod Browning, 1931*

I T TOOK A LONG TIME FOR Dracula to be made into a film. A list of early silent movies shows a number of films with vampire in the title, starting in about 1909 with *Vampires of the Coast*. None of these early 'vampire' films actually featured the creature, but rather played on the idea of 'vamp', meaning seductress. The early cinema was closely associated with the stage and popular theatre productions were often made into films. Bram Stoker established a performance copyright for his novel immediately after its publication and it was held by his widow until she licensed it to Hamilton Deane in 1924. The stage play ran throughout the world for another seven years before being made into a film. Universal Studios' legendary *Dracula*, directed by Tod Browning in 1931, was the first official film version of Stoker's book. But it wasn't the first vampire film.

The most famous unauthorised film version of *Dracula* is *Nosferatu*, a silent movie from 1922, directed by F. W. Murnau. It remains a deeply frightening movie. The story is more or less Stoker's *Dracula* though the names have been changed and some of the characters have been dropped or combined. The vampire is called Count Orlock and is played by a German actor named Max Schreck. A recent film called *Shadow of the Vampire* (2000), is predicated on the notion that Schreck was, in fact, a vampire. It is easy to believe while watching *Nosferatu*. Schreck's vampire is a different creature to the one that Stoker created. He is a monster, hunched and old, with a bald head and claw-like hands. His teeth stick out so that he looks like a large rat. Unlike the debonair aristocrat that would dominate twentieth century films, Orlock seems barely human. If anything, he is a throwback to the vampire legends of the eighteenth century. In the manner of German Expressionist films like the equally frightening *Cabinet of Dr Caligari*, lighting and shadows are used and sometimes the audience can only see the dark projection of this terrifying creature. Silent films can seem very antiquated to today's audiences but some, like *Nosferatu* will never lose their capacity to frighten.

In the early days of film, movies were sometimes lost. There were only so many copies around and if they all disappeared, there was no possibility of recovering them. It is estimated that more than 80 per cent of all silent movies were lost. *Nosferatu* itself came dangerously close to disappearing forever due to a legal suit brought by Bram Stoker's widow. She claimed that the story was too close to *Dracula* and she sued the small German studio that produced it. In 1925, a court concluded that the film was in fact an unauthorised version of the book, and ordered that all copies be destroyed. A few years later, Universal Studios obtained a copy but that too was destroyed. In the early 1930s, further copies were screened in the USA but these too were destroyed. Shorter versions and rough cuts existed and a very brief version was shown on television in the 1960s. Only one copy of the entire movie actually survived. In the early 1980s, it was restored and shown at the 1984 Berlin Film Festival. It was the first time in more than 50 years that anyone had seen it. It is now part of the public domain and can be downloaded free of charge.

Despite featuring an almost unrecognisable vampire, *Nosferatu* did introduce one important innovation to the vampire story. Not only was Orlock powerless in daylight, but sunlight was actually deadly for him. At the end of the movie, he is caught out while sucking the blood of the Mina character and is destroyed by the dawn's light. This new feature of vampire lore has been used regularly in films and books since *Nosferatu*.

But it was the first authorised version of *Dracula* that is generally considered the most important vampire film ever made. *Dracula*, directed by Tod Browning in 1931, featured an actor called Bela Lugosi whose vampire remains firmly in the popular imagination. Even in the wake of *Twilight*, it is Bela Lugosi whose look children will commandeer for Halloween costumes.

Bela Lugosi was almost fifty years old when
he began to play the role in a New York stage
production. His real name was Bela Blasko but
he took the name of the village where he grew up,
Lugos, as his stage name. Lugos, as it happens, is
only 50 kilometres from the Transylvanian border
so Lugosi brought considerable credibility to the
role. His Hungarian accent has become a hallmark
of vampires with lines like, 'I nev – air drink weh –
ine', and the line that he never actually said —
'I vant to suck your blood!'

Lugosi arrived in the United States in 1920.
He had been a member of the Hungarian Royal
Theatre and had appeared in films in Germany.
When he played his first roles in America, he spoke
virtually no English and simply memorised his
lines phonetically. His life changed forever when
he got the part of Dracula for the first American
production of the stage play. It ran for 40 weeks.
At the same time Lugosi was taking small parts in
films, and when Universal Studios decided to make
a film of *Dracula* in 1930, he was one of the actors
considered for the role. He nearly didn't get it.
Lon Chaney, the 'man of a thousand faces', was the

director's first choice. He had already played the
title roles in both *The Hunchback of Notre Dame*
(1923) and *The Phantom of the Opera* (1925). He
had also made a movie that owed something to the
vampire tradition called *London After Midnight*
(1927). The film is now lost, but the remaining
photographic stills show Chaney heavily made-up to
look like a living skeleton with a top hat, a wild grin,
and long white hair. The image has lasted where the
film hasn't. Chaney had actually signed the contract
to play Dracula, but died suddenly before filming
could begin. Lugosi was given the role immediately.

Like the novel, the film begins with the trip to
Dracula's castle, except this time it is Renfield
(the bug-eating lunatic in Stoker's novel) who
is making the journey. He meets Dracula and is
almost immediately set upon by female vampires,
the brides of Dracula. As in the novel, Dracula
then makes his way to England and begins to
prey on young women. Eventually he is foiled by
Van Helsing, who kills him by driving a wooden
stake through his heart. There is no return to
Transylvania and Dracula is killed in the basement
of a ruined abbey in England. Except for the

opening scene in Dracula's castle, the story follows the same plot as the stage play.

Sound was a relatively recent innovation in films when *Dracula* was made, and the acting style of many of the characters reflects the expressive gestures of silent film. Bela Lugosi's challenge was to redefine for the screen a role that he had played on stage hundreds of times. He must have been successful. The film was the top grossing movie for Universal Pictures in 1931, and for the first time since the beginning of the Depression in 1929, the studio made a profit.

Universal didn't immediately make a sequel. In this period, *Dracula* was the only vampire story, and it had already been filmed. Instead, Universal made a movie of the other horror story that came out of the Villa Diodati that stormy night in 1816. *Frankenstein*, starring Boris Karloff, was Universal's next horror hit. It wasn't until 1936 that the Dracula sequel appeared in the form of *Dracula's Daughter*. The film begins at the very moment *Dracula* ends, when Van Helsing, played by the same actor, comes forward to confess to Dracula's murder. The Count's daughter then appears to claim the body and the film then follows the familiar formula. Young women are attacked until the vampire dies, this time killed by a wooden arrow fired by her disgruntled servant. *Dracula's Daughter* was followed by *Son of Dracula* (1943) starring Lon Chaney Jr and *House of Dracula* (1945) with John Carradine. Bela Lugosi continued to play vampires and reprised his Dracula character in the comedy *Abbot and Costello Meet Frankenstein* in 1949. His last film was the legendary 'worst movie of all time', *Plan 9 from Outer Space* (1959), where he played, of course, a vampire. Lugosi actually died before filming began, but footage of him shot before his death was spliced into the film. Lugosi died in 1956 and was buried in his cape.

The popularity of vampires stretch from Polidori's Lord Ruthven to Meyer's Edward. There has only been one period where vampires seemed to fade somewhat from the public consciousness. From the end of the Second World War in 1945 to the late 1950s, vampires only appeared sporadically on film and in books. Science-fiction had become very popular in the cinema and so when vampires did appear it was often as aliens from other planets. Why, after such a long run, did the creature suddenly fade? There are several possibilities. Perhaps, they had simply finished a cycle of popularity. The end of the war provided something of a cultural break. Vampires might have seemed somewhat old-news as people looked ahead to a new period in the second half of the twentieth century. It is also possible that the Nazis represented a brand of murderous evil that was simply too close to the vampire story. It has also been speculated that the appearance of the nuclear bomb at the end of the war created an all too real monster that made the terror inspired by vampires seem redundant. In any case, it was only a short break, and when the vampire did reappear, it was in a spectacular fashion.

Hammer Horror

In 1958, a British movie company called Hammer Films released *Dracula*, which was renamed in the USA as *Horror of Dracula*. It was the first cinematic retelling of Bram Stoker's novel in more than two decades. By the time the first age of vampires on film had finished, the story had become a cliché ridiculed in comedy films. It would need something special to make it fresh for a new generation of filmgoers. In the late 1950s, colour was the feature that brought Dracula back. Gone were the dark Gothic sets and costumes. This was Dracula in vivid technicolour. Rich red blood flowed in virtually every scene and audiences were duly terrified.

Horror of Dracula, directed by Terrence Fisher, starred Christopher Lee in the title role. Lee's version of Dracula owed much to Bela Lugosi. He was tall, dark, charming, and utterly ruthless. For the first time, the sharp teeth became a distinguishing feature of the cinematic vampire. Stoker's story provides the basic outline but in this version, Jonathan Harker arrives at Dracula's castle under the premise that he is a librarian who has arrived to catalogue the books in the Count's library. He is, in fact, a vampire hunter intent on destroying Dracula. After managing to destroy Dracula's 'bride', he is turned into a vampire. His

friend and fellow vampire hunter, Dr Van Helsing,
arrives at the castle and is forced to drive a wooden
stake through his friend's heart. From this point,
the film moves into more predictable territory as
Dracula terrorises Harker's fiancée and her sister.
The vampire's inevitable destruction at the end of
the film takes places after a dramatic battle between
the Count and Van Helsing. The vampire hunter
finally tears down the curtains in Dracula's dining
room and forces him into the sunlight by holding
up two large candlesticks in the form of a cross. The
vampire shrivels up and turns to dust. As the film
ends, only his ring remains, glittering in the deadly
morning light. The film was very successful and
Hammer continued to produce sequels throughout
the 60s and 70s. Some were okay, some were
atrocious, but many are now cult favourites among
horror movie buffs.

*F*OR A CERTAIN GENERATION *of film fans, Christopher Lee will always be Dracula, with Peter Cushing as his arch-enemy, Dr Van Helsing. The two actors first appeared together in Lawrence Olivier's celebrated 1948 version of* Hamlet. *Both actors later appeared in the* Star Wars *movie series: Lee as Count Dooku in Episode II and Cushing as Tarkin in Episode IV. Both actors found it difficult to escape their association with vampires however, and like Bela Lugosi before them, they often found themselves reprising the roles that made them famous.*

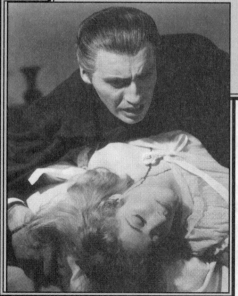

Christopher Lee as Dracula in Dracula: Prince of Darkness *(1966)*   85

6

Try the Holy Water, Death Breath:

Vampire Films Part Two

Sleep all day. Party all night. It's fun to be a vampire.

Edgar Frog: 'You did the right thing by calling us. Does your brother sleep a lot?'

Sam Emerson: 'Yeah, all day.'

Alan Frog: 'Does the sunlight freak him out?'

Sam Emerson: 'Uh, he wears sunglasses in the house.'

Edgar Frog: 'Bad breath, long fingernails?'

Sam Emerson: 'Yeah, his fingernails are a little bit longer, um, he always had bad breath, though.'

Alan Frog: 'He's a vampire all right.'

Edgar Frog: 'All right, here's what you do: get yourself a good sharp stake and drive it right through his heart.'

Sam Emerson: 'I can't do that; he's my brother.'

Alan Frog: 'OK, we'll come over and do it for you.'

Sam Emerson: 'No!'

Edgar Frog: 'You'd better get yourself a garlic T-shirt, buddy, or it's your funeral.'

— The Lost Boys, *directed by Joel Schumacher, 1987*

A FILM THAT APPEARED in 1987 was the beginning of a whole new era in vampire stories. In *The Lost Boys*, the gloomy old Transylvanian count was replaced by a young punk with dyed-blond spiked hair, a motorcycle, a beautiful girlfriend, and a taste for fun — along with a taste for blood. David, played by a young Kiefer Sutherland, is a cool vampire. He and his friends look like a glam metal band. If Stephenie Meyer's Edward is the handsome and slightly mysterious nice boy at school, Sutherland's David is the bad boy. He is smart, tough, and very dangerous.

David and the other teenage vampires live in the ruins of an old hotel that ended up at the bottom of a cliff after an earthquake. There is a large poster of The Doors lead singer, Jim Morrison, candles, curtains, and plenty of old furniture. It is the ultimate vampire lair. During the night-time hours, David and his friends terrorise the small town of Santa Clara, a California beachside community. At the beginning of the film, they walk through the fairgrounds, intimidating people until they are thrown out. Before the audience knows that they are vampires, they look like a gang. Only when the security guard is attacked by something that swoops down on him does it become clear that David is more than just a local hood. All over the town, flyers are posted that feature the faces of children that have disappeared. Something very sinister is afoot in Santa Clara.

Into the midst of all of this evil comes Sam (Corey Haim), his big brother, Michael (Jason Patric) and their mum who has just separated from their father. She is moving in with the boys' grandfather who lives in the town. The boys go to the fairgrounds soon after their arrival and Michael falls in love with a mysterious girl named Star (Jami Gertz). The girl turns out to be David's girlfriend. Michael falls in with the vampires and begins to act very strangely. Meanwhile his brother Sam has met two young brothers, Edgar and Allan Frog, who claim to be vampire hunters. Sam is dubious, but when his brother starts to exhibit some of the signs of vampirism, he asks for their help.

To save his brother the head vampire must be killed. Sam and Michael's mother has been dating a man called Max and at first they suspect that he might be the one. In a very funny scene at dinner, they put garlic on his food, spray him with holy water and put a mirror in his face to see if there is a reflection. The only hint that they might be on the right track is Max's insistence that he be invited into the house, something Sam doesn't notice.

Michael begins to resist becoming a 'full' vampire and rescues Star from the vampire cave while David and his friends are sleeping during the day. Sam and the Frog brothers stake one of the vampires in the same scene, and are chased from the cave by David. That night, the vampires attack Sam at Michael's house. All of the vampires, including

David, are killed but Michael remains a vampire. Max and the boys' mother appear and Max reveals that he is, in fact, the head vampire. He wanted 'his' boys, the vampires, to have a mum and thought that he could be a father to Michael and Sam. 'Great,' says one of the Frog brothers, 'The blood sucking Brady Bunch.' As Max attempts to bite the boys' mother, their grandfather drives his truck into the living room and fires a large stake into Max who disappears into flames and smoke. The grandfather is an eccentric man who lurks in the background of the film. At the end however, he stands drinking a root beer in the ruins of his house and says, 'One thing about Santa Clara I never could stomach, all the damn vampires.' He has known what was going on all along.

The Lost Boys is an entertaining film. Kiefer Sutherland makes a convincingly appealing bloodsucker and the slightly sleazy beachside town is a surprisingly good setting for a vampire film. The combination of horror and comedy is something that is often attempted by filmmakers but rarely succeeds. *The Lost Boys* is a funny film with plenty of sharp dialogue. Corey Feldman, as Edgar

Frog, nearly steals the show with lines like, 'Try the holy water, death breath.' But this is still a genuinely frightening film. There is nothing funny about David and his gang as they abduct and murder their victims by night. The final scene is violent and gory as David is impaled on moose antlers while another vampire is fried in a bathtub filled with holy water.

The Lost Boys remains an iconic 1980s film. The director, Joel Schumacher, set out to update the vampire story and make it relevant to young audiences. But it is worth noting that, though the film seems to be miles away from more traditional vampire stories, it is actually a loose retelling of *Dracula*. The Frog brothers are vampire hunters in the Van Helsing mode who try to save Michael, the Jonathan Harker character, from becoming a vampire. Many of the hallmarks of vampire lore appear in this film. Wooden stakes, garlic, mirrors, crosses and holy water are used to battle vampires. The key mistake made by Sam in inviting Max into his house is part of a tradition that goes back to the nineteenth century. Vampires can only enter a house if they are invited to do so.

Two other films appeared in the late 1980s that have remained popular. *Near Dark* (1987), which was conceived as a western but morphed into a vampire film, came out in the same year as *The Lost Boys*. Again, a character is initiated into a vampire gang, only to turn against it and escape with the girl in the end. *Fright Night* (1985) is a classic 1980s horror film that continues to terrify anyone brave enough to watch it. The invitation into the house is a component of *Fright Night*, and the film features a Van Helsing character in the guise of a late-night TV personality who hosts a horror movie program. Vampires were being reinvented for a new generation, but the same basic elements remained in place. In 1992, director Francis Ford Coppola decided to attempt a new version of something very old in cinema. He decided to make a film of the novel by Bram Stoker.

Bram Stoker's Dracula may be the most faithful film version of the novel ever to hit the screen, but Francis Ford Coppola seems to have thrown a little bit of everything into his movie. Ironically, considering the title, the opening scene does not appear in the novel. Prince Dracula is off to fight the Turkish invaders. His beloved wife, Elizabeth, is overcome with fear that her husband will be killed in battle. He is victorious, but the Turks send a false message to his wife that says he has died. She leaps to her death from the castle walls. When Dracula returns, he is told by the priest that his wife cannot be buried in hallowed ground because she has committed suicide. The Prince takes exception to this and drives his sword into a cross in the abbey while renouncing his religion. The room fills with blood and the vampire is born.

Coppola has employed a bit of Vlad the Impaler's story to create the basis for a romance that will span the centuries. Dracula's wife is played by Wynona Ryder who also plays Mina, Jonathan Harker's fiancée. Vlad the Impaler's wife did in fact commit suicide, but probably out of fear rather than grief. The name Elizabeth might be a reference to Elizabeth Bathory, the original model for female vampires. In any case, it becomes clear that this is a film that is not going to be constrained by Stoker's novel. Jonathan Harker is played by Keanu Reeves. His trip to Dracula's castle at the beginning of the film pays tribute to the original *Dracula* film

starring Bela Lugosi. The steps up to the castle
look almost identical to those in the older film. Gary
Oldman, who plays Dracula, even delivers Lugosi's
timeless line, 'I never,' he says, pausing briefly,
'drink...wine.' Although it is not a comedy, it does
have a light moment in the castle when Dracula
says to Harker, 'They say you are a man of good...
taste.' But Oldman doesn't look anything like Bela
Lugosi. His vampire, at least at the beginning
of the film, is more of a tribute to the monster in
Murnau's *Nosferatu*. Coppola even uses shadows
periodically in a manner that recalls that film.

The film unfolds more or less like the book,
though Coppola has created a romance between
Mina and the vampire that is certainly not a feature
of the novel. Some critics see the original story as
being about that fear that English women will fall
in love with foreign men. Coppola makes this the
central theme of the film. Jonathan Harker is
a decent, well-intentioned young man, but he is
no match for the vampire when Dracula arrives in
England. Gary Oldman's vampire looks like the
lost member of the Rolling Stones. He wears a top
hat over long dark hair and hides his eyes, in part,

behind small, circular, blue-tinted glasses. Mina is overwhelmed by both his charm and, in one memorable scene, his pet wolf. She begins to feel a sense of recognition when she is with him. Dracula, for his part, wants to bite her and make her a vampire but cannot bring himself to do so. Despite him having killed her best friend, Lucy, Mina feels sorry for Dracula and so does the audience. The ruthless killer of the novel and most early films has now been replaced by a character who is still bad, but not without some redeeming features. By 1992, audiences wanted a vampire that they could feel at least a hint of sympathy for and Gary Oldman recreates Dracula in this mould.

There are two good reasons to watch *Bram Stoker's Dracula*. There has never been a better Van Helsing than Anthony Hopkins. Stoker realised that a person who hunts vampires would have to be a genuine eccentric. Most films have made the mistake of turning this character into a cold, dispassionate scientist. Hopkins' Van Helsing is exactly the kind of person you would expect to be hunting the undead. He is brilliant, resourceful and a little bit unbalanced. The other character who comes to life in this film is the patient in the lunatic asylum, Renfield. Other directors have either dropped this character altogether or greatly reduced his role in the story. The part of Renfield is played brilliantly by the singer Tom Waits, who engages in a classic bit of dialogue with Richard E. Grant's Dr Jack Seward. The doctor has been watching Renfield eat bugs when the patient makes a request:

Renfield: Oh, yes. A kitten. I beg you. A little playful kitten. Something I can teach. Something I can feed. No one would refuse me a kitten.
Doctor Seward: Wouldn't you prefer a cat?
Renfield: Oh, yes, a big cat! My salvation depends upon it!
Doctor Seward: Your salvation?
Renfield: Yes! I need lives. I need lives for the master!
Doctor Seward: What? What master?
Renfield: The master will come, and he has promised to make me immortal!
Doctor Seward: How?
[Renfield suddenly attacks Seward and the guards rush in to subdue him]

Renfield: The blood is the life! The blood is the life!

Tom Waits' expression as he begs Seward for 'big cat', and Richard E. Grant's bemused reaction both make for a great moment in the film.

Another vampire film appeared in 1992. The focus this time was on the hunter rather than the creature, but this was no mad scientist. Instead, it was a cheerleader named Buffy whose adventures would continue on television. The 1990s also saw the appearance of *Blade* in 1998, another vampire-hunter film that would spawn a series of sequels. Blade first appeared in the Marvel comic, *The Tomb of Dracula*. In the film, he is a 'Daywalker' — half vampire, half human. He has the power of a vampire but his mission is to protect humans. *Blade*, unlike *Buffy the Vampire Slayer* and Bram Stoker's *Dracula*, is an action film with dazzling special effects and weapons. Throughout the nineties, this genre became increasingly popular and it was inevitable that a vampire-related action hero would appear. The *Underworld* series, dealing with the battle between vampires and werewolves, is another series in the action/horror genre.

The current wave of vampire movies includes the full range of vampire possibilities. The spoof *Lesbian Vampire Killers* was released in 2009, and the sinister *Let the Right One In*, in 2008, a Swedish film combining romantic and grunge elements. Another film in the *Twilight* series also arrived to much fanfare in 2009. The early 2010 release of *Daybreakers*, was a science-fiction vampire film in the tradition of *I am Legend*. The Gothic romance of *Twilight* may be leading the current crop of vampire films, but it seems that there is plenty of room for vampires of every kind.

Wesley Snipes as Blade in Blade Trinity *(2004)*

*T*HE *1971 FILM* LET'S SCARE
Jessica to Death, *directed by John
Hancock, is considered by many to
be one of the scariest films ever made.
A woman who has had a nervous
breakdown leaves the city for a farmhouse
in the country. She goes with her husband
and his friend, but meet a hippie girl called
Emily who lives in the house. Jessica begins
to hear Emily's voice in her head and it seems
that Emily may be a vampire or something
equally spooky. But the scary thing about the
film is that the viewer is never sure what
is real and what is simply a component of
Jessica's madness. There are some connections
will Sheridan Le Fanu's* Carmilla, *and*
Let's Scare Jessica to Death *remains a cult
classic.*

When Morbius Met Spider-Man:

Vampire Comics

7

Vampires are prohibited...

Spider-Man : (He's going for my throat with his fangs. Then I was right though I didn't dare believe it till now)

You are some kind of vampire!!!

Morbius: Vampire? Yes, I suppose your tiny mind would label me thus. But what do simple epithets mean to me? I am more than any name, beyond any epithet!!!

— The Amazing Spider-Man #101, *Marvel Comics, 1971*

NOT SO LONG AGO IN THE USA, parents, teachers, and community leaders decided that enough was enough. They knew that a danger was lurking that needed to be dealt with. But while adults understood the nature of this danger, their children did not; every last cent of their pocket money was being spent on it. The children needed to be rescued from the clutches of the people behind this scourge. So in towns and suburbs, massive bonfires were lit, sending smoke high into the afternoon sky as the children watched the sources of their pleasure curl up and disappear in flames. What would life be like without their... vampire comics?

It is hard to imagine how comics could have once created such a storm in the community. In the early 1950s, scenes like the one above were repeated over and over throughout America as communities came together to destroy the offending items. Books and countless newspaper articles were written about the effects of comic books on children, and hysteria ruled the day as politicians were elected promising to ban them. One man, Estes Kefauver, who built his career on the comic book issue, could have easily become president had it not been for the meteoric rise of John F. Kennedy in the late 1950s.

Comics had always been controversial. Early newspaper comic strips, such as *Hogan's Alley* and *The Katzenjammer Twins*, were populated by trouble-making kids. As early as 1909, articles began to appear condemning the strips and suggesting that they were encouraging delinquency among the nation's youth. The first comic books began to appear in the early 1930s. At first they were just collections of popular comic strips but slowly collections of original stories began to appear. One of the earliest was a comic called *New Fun* that featured, among others, a regular story called

Dr Occult, the Ghost Detective. In issue #6, Dr Occult fought and defeated a vampire. This was the first appearance of the creature in an American comic. It was created by Joe Shuster and Jerry Seigel, the pair who, in 1938, would create the most important superhero of all time — Superman.

In April of 1939, another iconic superhero appeared in *Detective Comics #*27. He wore a cape and was known as Batman. Although not directly inspired by vampire stories, Batman comics have always been had a distinctly Gothic tone. In his fifth appearance in the comic later that year (*Detective Comics #*31), Batman fought a villain called The Monk, a vampire. The Monk had kidnapped Bruce Wayne's fiancée and taken her to Paris. To rescue her, Batman uses a range of gadgets including, in their first appearances, the Bat-erang and the Bat plane. He rescues her but does not destroy The Monk. That happens in the next issue when Batman, uncharacteristically, uses a handgun to fire a silver bullet into the heart of his adversary. For reasons that will soon be obvious, Batman did not fight another vampire until *Detective Comics #*455 which appeared in 1976!

Today, most people associate comic books with superheroes. While those characters have dominated the medium, there have been periods where other genres were more popular. In the late 1940s, a company called B&I Publishing launched a comic called *Adventures into the Unknown*, which featured illustrated horror stories. Often they were based on Gothic tales from the nineteenth century, and vampire stories were regularly featured. Two years later, in 1950, EC comics started *Crypt of Terror*, which soon became *Tales from the Crypt*, the most famous horror comic. It was later made into a film and a television show. The comic featured three hosts: Crypt Keeper, the Old Witch, and Vault Keeper, one of whom would introduce each story. The stories were seriously frightening and the accompanying pictures were often graphically violent. One horror comic, *Eerie*, told the Dracula story in its eighth issue.

Two other genres were also very popular at the time. Romance comics were popular with girls and many of the stories were surprisingly risqué for the time. Crime comics also sold well but their extreme violence began to attract the attention of community leaders. A leading psychologist named Frederic Wertham published a book called *Seduction of the Innocent* in 1954. His thesis was that the violence depicted in comic books was a direct cause of the increase in youth crime. Very few of his theories were supported with any kind of real evidence and he seemed to begin with the premise that comic books were somehow inherently evil. America in the 1950s was a conservative place and his ideas were taken very seriously. At the time, a subcommittee of the US Senate, the Senate Subcommittee on Juvenile Delinquency, had been convened to address the problem of youth crime. Wertham was one of their star witnesses. The publicity sparked a veritable comic book witch-hunt. Communities ran programs where they collected as many comic books as they could and burned them in huge bonfires. Often these events were organised by the students themselves and all of them attracted publicity. Large groups of students would be asked to pledge that they would no longer read comics as a match was lit. For many recent immigrants to the USA, particularly those who had arrived fleeing the book-burning Nazis, the spectacle was disturbing.

When shops refused to carry horror, crime and romance titles, the comic publishing industry decided to take action. They came together and formed the Comics and Magazine Association of America (CMAA). The publishers decided that they would need to regulate themselves or face a complete ban on comics. In many places in the USA, government bodies were already making laws that censored comics. The CMAA created a code, the Comics Code Authority, that all members were obliged to follow. The code included the following:

Scenes dealing with, or instruments associated with, walking dead, torture, vampires and vampirism, ghouls, cannibalism, werewolfism are prohibited.

The ban on vampires was thus absolute; vampires could not appear in comic books. When the code came into effect, horror comics disappeared immediately and crime comics became much less interesting. Romance comics, now devoid of any controversial content and with new stories of wholesome, well-behaved teenage couples, also lost most of their readership. The powers that sought to ban comics were largely successful, but the code had an interesting side effect. Teenagers who had previously read thrilling tales of horror, crime, and romance in the comics, found the cleaned-up versions dull. For entertainment, they turned to a new medium. It was called television.

For the next 17 years, virtually no vampires appeared in mainstream comics. In 1971, the comic code was updated. The world had changed considerably in the 1960s and the CMAA realised that they had to move with the times. The code remained, as it does today, quite strict on many subjects, but it did revise the section on certain horror characters:

Vampires, ghouls and werewolves shall be permitted to be used when handled in the classic tradition such as Frankenstein, Dracula, *and other high calibre literary works written by Edgar Allen Poe, Saki (H.H. Munro), Conan Doyle, and other respected authors whose works are read in schools throughout the world.*

The Tomb of Dracula

Marvel Comics, the home of *Spider-Man* and *The Hulk*, responded immediately and launched *The Tomb of Dracula*. To make sure that the connection with the 'classic tradition' was obvious, the story began with a man called Frank Drake who learns that he is a descendant of the original Count Dracula. He decides to make his fortune in Transylvania turning the Count's castle into a tourist attraction. He takes along his friend Clifton Graves who makes a bad mistake once inside the castle. Graves finds an old skeleton with a stake stuck between its ribs, which he removes and tosses away. Dracula soon rises once again. Throughout the comic, Stoker's *Dracula* is retold as a back-story. *The Tomb of Dracula* lasted for 70 issues until it was discontinued in 1979.

Throughout the 1960s, Spider-Man had been Marvel's most popular character. Soon after the ban was lifted, Spider-Man found himself locked in battle with a vampire called Morbius. Morbius is interesting because he is not in tradition of the classic Dracula. Doctor Michael Morbius is a chemist who finds out that he has a rare blood disease. He tries to cure it using vampire bats and electroshock therapy, only to find that he has become a vampire. Issue #101 of *The Amazing Spider-Man*, featuring Morbius' first appearance, is notable also for being the first Spider-Man episode not written by its creator, Stan Lee. Morbius would continue to appear in various Marvel comics over the years. There is a long-standing rumour that Sam Raimi, the director of the Spider-Man movies, would like to introduce Morbius into one of his films.

Vampires came and went in Marvel comics throughout the 1970s, but in the 1983 issue #62 of *Doctor Strange: Master of the Mystic Arts*, the Doctor, an enduring Marvel character, discovers a magic ritual that will rid the world of vampires. He performs it and the world is finally free of the bloodsucking menace. Vampires were absent from Marvel until 1989 when Morbius, who somehow survived the spell, reappeared in another *Doctor Strange* comic. Morbius finally got his own comic in 1992.

Vampirella

The longest running vampire comic, however, featured a female vampire. *Vampirella* first appeared in 1969. By the late 1960s, publishers wishing to avoid the code published black and white comics in 'magazines'. The character Vampirella, a vampire from outer space, first appeared as a host, introducing a series of illustrated horror stories involving female characters. She then became the main character for an amazing run that lasted for 112 issues over 14 years. Through the years she battled all manner of enemies. At one point, she went back in time and followed Dracula through many of the sequences in Bram Stoker's novel. A forgettable film version of *Vampirella* appeared in a straight-to-video release in 1996. The comics have been reprinted several times.

It is not so surprising that vampires have reappeared in comics regularly since the early days of the form. Superhero stories, which have dominated the medium, are usually predicated on a character who appears to be human but has extraordinary abilities. The vampire, the most important Gothic character of the nineteenth century, was ready-made to play a part in one of the twentieth century's most significant artistic mediums. Vampires continue to inspire graphic-novel writers in this century and it is unlikely that they will ever completely disappear from comics. Unless, of course, someone decides once again that vampire stories are going to lead children directly into a life of crime.

IN 1991, A GRAPHIC NOVEL appeared that paired the legendary comic book hero, Batman, with Dracula. It has always been noted that Batman owes something to Bram Stoker's creation. His cape, the association with bats, and the urban Gothic quality of the comic have always suggested a similarity. Red Rain *explores the idea of vampirism. Though Dracula is the bad guy, the novel has more in common with the scientific vampire stories like* I am Legend *that appeared in the 1950s. Batman becomes a vampire but is helped by a female vampire called Tania who has created a blood substitute to stop her from killing people. Without spoiling the ending, Batman's new-found strength as a vampire means that he can take on the all-powerful Dracula.* Red Rain *is considered one of the best Batman graphic novels. It is now available with the two sequels in a single book.*

Night Stalkers and Cheerleaders: Vampires on Television

8

A vampire with a soul — how lame is that?

'It's my first day! I was afraid that I was gonna be behind in all my classes, that I wouldn't make any friends, that I would have last month's hair. I didn't think there'd be vampires on campus. And I don't care!'

— Buffy The Vampire Slayer, *Season One, Episode One.*

BELA LUGOSI, WHO WAS ONE OF the earliest
actors to play Dracula on the stage and in
film, was also the first vampire on television.
Only two years before his death, he appeared on
a show called *You Asked For It*. He recreated
a scene from his most famous movie and was then
interviewed by the host. It was the beginning of a
long relationship between the undead and the most
significant entertainment form of the late twentieth
century.

Early television, like the early cinema, borrowed
heavily from theatre. Theatre groups often
performed short or abridged plays on programs that
featured a new play every week. In 1955,

a show called *Matinee Theatre* featured a version of *Dracula* based on the stage play. It starred John Carradine, who had played the part on the stage. He had also played a vampire in several films. Horror shows of this type were popular in the early days of television and vampires made regular appearances.

In 1964, two shows were launched. They were both comedy programs and both featured vampires. One was *The Addams Family*, which was based on a popular cartoon that appeared regularly in *The New Yorker*. The idea was a family, all of whom resemble common horror characters, who alternately perplex and terrify their neighbours. It started running in the magazine in 1938 and lasted 50 years. The television show starred Carolyn Jones who played the vampire-like mother, Morticia Addams. The show lasted two years but has been revived many times on television and in movies.

The other show that appeared that year was *The Munsters*. It was more or less the same idea except that the Munsters were not quite as wealthy as the Addams family and not quite as smooth. But the basic joke was the same. In most episodes, the families are caught up somehow with 'normal' members of society who don't understand or are frightened by them. *The Munsters* was a slightly hipper show that featured musical guests. It rated higher but lasted, like *The Addams Family*, for only two years. It has also been revived many times on television and in films. *The Munsters* featured two vampires, Lily Munster, the mother, and her father, Grandpa Munster. In one episode, it was revealed that Grandpa Munster was, in fact, Count Dracula.

Dark Shadows

But none of these TV vampires would be as big as the one that appeared in 1967. A year earlier, a daytime soap opera called *Dark Shadows* began. It was similar to other soapies in that it had a large family at its centre and featured all of the usual plot devices — infidelity, secrets, and shock revelations. The family, the Collins', were an old American family and the story was mainly set in their 300-year-old mansion, Collinswood. The concept was a soapie with Gothic overtones.

A ghost appeared in an early episode and most of the action revolved around a murder that had taken place some time earlier. It wasn't very popular. Daytime soap fans are a very particular audience, and *Dark Shadows* was struggling in the ratings. The television network began to discuss cancelling the show.

At the last minute, the writers decided to introduce a new character that they hoped would create a bit of buzz and get people interested in the show. They hired Jonathan Frid, a Canadian stage actor best known for Shakespearean roles to play a vampire who returns to the house. They had no intention of keeping him in the show. Barnabas Collins' appearance was to be a publicity stunt and nothing more. The effect was electric. Daytime audiences may not have been sure about a haunted-house story but they couldn't get enough of the vampire. He became so popular that he remained the main character for another four years and almost 1000 episodes until the show was cancelled.

Barnabas' back-story became an important story-line for the show. A séance took the cast back to the 1790s where they played the part of their ancestors. The audience learned that Barnabas had been tricked into a marriage with a witch. But when he found out that she had used magic, he shot her. With her dying words she put a curse on him, and he was attacked by a vampire bat that killed him. He arose soon afterwards. When the story returned to the present, the audience was more sympathetic to Barnabas. *Twilight* readers looking for an early version of the sensitive Edward need look no further than this vampire.

The show has been revived several times but never with the same success. Barnabas Collins remains one of the most popular vampires — Johnny Depp has said that Barnabas is his favourite television character of all time. There has been a *Dark Shadows* film in the works for several years and the rumour is that it will be directed by Tim Burton. Johnny Depp is set to play his hero, Barnabas, and will no doubt his add own unique touch to the character.

Not long after the final episode of the original series of *Dark Shadows*, another television show appeared involving vampires. *The Night Stalker* began as a made-for-TV movie but became a television series in 1974 under the title *Kolchak: The Night Stalker*. The title character, Carl Kolchak, is a Las Vegas reporter who follows up unsolved crimes, usually murders that have stumped the police. These crimes always involve some kind of supernatural element. The original telemovie, which was written by Richard Matheson, the author of *I am Legend*, was about a vampire committing murders in Las Vegas. The television show only featured one episode (episode four) about vampires, but it inspired another much more popular show that dealt with the supernatural. *The X-Files*, though ostensibly about UFOs, featured vampires in several episodes throughout its nine-season run on television that began in 1993. The investigators this time were FBI agents following up strange and difficult to explain crimes. Episodes such as *Bad Blood* from Season Five dealt with vampires and vampire culture in detail.

Buffy

With the exception of *Dark Shadows*, vampires and television had a somewhat uncertain relationship until the 1990s. A number of series were attempted, but most, including the popular *Forever Knight*, only lasted for a season or two. That is, until a vampire-hunting cheerleader from a moderately successful 1992 movie reappeared on television in 1997. The age of Buffy had begun.

Buffy The Vampire Slayer is one of those rare television shows that are more than simply popular. Buffy, it is fair to say, has become a cultural icon. The show lasted seven seasons but continues to have a life outside of television that includes books, comics, games, toys and clothing. Universities offered courses on *Buffy* and many scholarly articles have been written on the topic. There have been conferences devoted to *Buffy* and its spinoff, *Angel*.

The main character, Buffy Summers, combined the name of a stereotypical American cheerleader with the surname shared with Montague Summers, the eccentric monk who wrote many books about vampires in the early twentieth century. The show changed considerably throughout its run on television. The comedy became more pronounced and the stories became increasingly dark. It featured a winning combination of high school drama, sitcom and horror. The story is simple. Buffy is a 'slayer' — one of a long line of women whose task is to fight evil, which usually takes the form of vampires. Her seemingly quiet Californian town, Sunnydale, sits on top of the 'Hellmouth', an area of supernatural activity, and is therefore a portal for vampires and other monsters. Buffy, along with her watcher, Giles, best friend Willow, and the hapless Xander, battles against the forces of evil. Naturally, Buffy also has romantic relationships and these became increasingly central as the series progressed. In particular, her relationships with Angel, the vampire with a soul, and the English punk vampire Spike, provide another dimension to the story. Part of the tension in the show is built on Buffy coming to terms with her role as a slayer, and how to balance it with the normal life of a young woman.

Buffy uses the traditional wooden stake to destroy vampires. Like most stories of the undead, the creature is reinvented to suit the purposes of the story. The universe of evil that Buffy battles is a complicated one, and is revealed slowly throughout the seasons. But like most vampire stories, Buffy borrows heavily from earlier tales. The vampire connoisseur will see elements of films like *The Lost Boys* and *Fright Night* along with traces of Anne Rice's novels. In one memorable episode, however, Buffy meets the most famous vampire of them all: Count Dracula.

By Season five, Buffy had met all manner of vampires and many other kinds of monsters. The first episode of Season five, *Buffy vs Dracula* is something of tribute to the most important vampire story. After defeating several run-of-the-mill vampires in the Sunnydale cemetery, Buffy finds herself face-to-face with the Count. Earlier in the show, lightning flashes over a Gothic mansion as two movers lift a crate filled with earth from a truck. 'I am Dracula', says the Count with the regulation Eastern European accent. 'Get out,' says Buffy before a quick fade to a commercial break.

The next scene finds Buffy's friends, the 'scooby gang', discussing Dracula. Buffy's boyfriend becomes annoyed when Buffy seems to have found the Count very attractive. Her watcher, Giles, makes a Van Helsing-like observation: 'The secret to defeating him is separating the fact from the fiction.' The episode then explores some of the elements of the Dracula story. Xander becomes the Renfield character. He is mesmerised by Dracula and spends most of the episode eating bugs and proclaiming the power of the 'master'. Buffy falls into the Mina role and is visited in her bedroom by the Count who arrives in the form of a green mist. The cynical Spike notes that Dracula owes him money and that his fame has made things difficult for vampires. 'Everyone knows how to kill us,' he reports. Buffy's boyfriend and Giles become the vampire hunters until Giles falls under the spell of the 'brides of Dracula', Jonathan Harker style. At the end, Buffy gets fed up with Dracula and dispatches him in her usual manner, with a wooden stake. As she walks away, he begins to reappear only to find himself staked again. 'You think I don't watch your movies?' says Buffy. 'You always come back.' A witty end to a witty episode that is as much about the Dracula myth as it is about Buffy's battle with the Count.

Until *Buffy The Vampire Slayer,* television vampires hadn't always fared as well as the networks might have wished. But in the wake of her success and the more recent success of shows like *True Blood* and *The Vampire Diaries*, it seems as though vampires have finally found their place in this medium.

And Buffy found a place for women in the vampire genre. Genres only last if they can remain relevant, and by 1990 the vampire story was in serious danger of disappearing if it couldn't find a more interesting place for its female characters. The helpless screaming victim and the young lovely besotted by Dracula's 'foreign' charms were becoming very tired as the vampire headed towards a new century. The female vampire, largely created by Sheridan Le Fanu, had also slipped into a male fantasy cliché. When Buffy appeared with her wooden stake, it signalled the beginning of a new era. She was smart, sexy, and dangerous in a fight. From now, the Van Helsing role could be played by a clever young woman with great dress sense. Though Stephenie Meyer's Bella is no vampire hunter, not in the traditional sense anyway, she remains part of the tradition begun by Buffy.

THE SIMPSONS' *1993 HALLOWEEN special, the fourth* Treehouse of Horror, *featured three stories, the third of which was a vampire story. Mr Burns has bought the local blood bank and invited the Simpson family to his house in 'Pennsylvania' for a midnight meal. When he answers the door, he looks like Gary Oldman at the beginning of* Bram Stoker's Dracula. *Homer makes fun of his hair and the whole family is served blood in wineglasses. 'Yah, but it's free blood!' says Homer. After Bart becomes a vampire, the parody shifts to* The Lost Boys *and Lisa finds Bart and his friends floating outside her window urging her to join them. It is a witty episode that pokes fun at the two films and the vampire genre in general.*

9

Legends and Lots: A Few Vampire Novels Later

He was brilliant…and perfect…and beautiful…and possibly able to lift full-sized vans with one hand…

About three things I was absolutely positive. First, Edward was a vampire. Second, there was part of him — and I didn't know how dominant that part might be — that thirsted for my blood. And third, I was unconditionally and irrevocably in love with him.

— Twilight *by Stephenie Meyer*

THE STORY OF THE VAMPIRE IS THE story of the stranger who comes among us. But what if *we* were the strangers in a world populated by the undead? In 1954, a novel appeared that turned the typical vampire story inside out. It is a book that has been filmed many times, most recently in a version starring Will Smith. Written by Richard Matheson, the book is *I am Legend*. It is the story of a man called Robert Neville who is the only human survivor of a plague that has turned everyone else into a vampire. When the novel begins, he is going through his nightly ritual of barricading himself into his house. When the sun sets, vampires appear outside calling for him to surrender. They try to gain entry to his house and the female vampires try to entice him to open his door. One of the vampires is a former neighbour, Ben Cortman, who calls out to him by name. Neville spends his days collecting food and maintaining his house. He also murders vampires as they sleep during the day.

In a series of the flashbacks, the reader learns about how the vampire plague began and how Neville lost his wife and daughter. Most of the dead were thrown into large burning pits so that they would not return as vampires. Neville puts his wife in a grave but when she returns he is forced to kill her with a stake through the heart. He is distressed by the memory and his nights are spent drinking to alleviate his loneliness and fear. Neville himself is immune to the virus. He believes that a bite from a vampire bat in Panama when he was younger has caused his immunity. His curiosity about the nature of the disease leads to a number of experiments. He eventually determines that it is a germ that is the source of the condition but has no idea what to do with this information.

Towards the end of the novel, he spots a woman, Ruth, while he is out during the day. He chases her and takes her back to his house. Noticing her aversion to garlic, he becomes suspicious that she is infected. When he tries to check her blood, she attacks him with a hammer and knocks him out. He awakes to find a note that tells him she is indeed infected, but that there are many like her who have found a way to live with the illness. Neville has been killing real vampires, but he has also killed many people who are simply infected, including Ruth's husband. The infected have sent her as a spy and plan to capture Neville. She warns him to escape but he doesn't and is eventually captured. On the eve of his execution, Ruth visits him and gives him suicide pills so that he can avoid an unpleasant death. At the end of the novel, he looks out the window and sees fear on the faces of the people outside the prison. They are scared of him and he realises that he has become the deadly creature. Vampires aren't legends — he is the legend.

I am Legend is a short and very entertaining story that falls somewhere between horror and science-fiction. It is also a novel that is about the vampire story as much as it is about vampires. Neville uses garlic and crosses to hold off the vampires. Later in the novel, he attempts to figure out whether or not there is a 'scientific' basis to their effectiveness. He asks an interesting question. Would a Muslim or Jewish vampire be afraid of a cross? Some of the most exciting scenes in the story unfold as Neville rushes back to his house at nightfall. Sunlight is deadly to the vampires in the story and this is another element that Neville explores, using a microscope and blood samples. He refers to Bram Stoker's *Dracula* but eventually throws the book across the room, concluding:

That was what the situation had been. Something black and of the night had come crawling out of the Middle Ages. Something with no framework or credulity, something that had been consigned, fact and figure, to the pages of imaginative literature. Vampires were passé: Summers' idylls; or Stoker's melodramatics; or a brief inclusion in the Britannica; *or grist for the pulp writer's mill; or raw material for the B-film factories. A tenuous legend passed from century to century.*

Well, it was true.

I am Legend appeared at the beginning of the Cold War. In the early fifties, the fear of a nuclear war was growing. The idea that humanity could be wiped out is the basis of the novel. Germ warfare and its alleged use in the Second World War and the Korean War was also an issue at the time.

I am Legend is set twenty years in the future and an unnamed war has taken place. There is some possibility that the germ has been released as a weapon

But the most interesting component of the novel is the question that it poses about the nature of vampire stories. The vampire is feared because it is an outsider, a mysterious creature who threatens our idea of humanity. Richard Matheson turns the story around and opens the door for a whole new kind of vampire story where humans and vampires begin to co-exist in a world less certain and less secure about its future.

Salem's Lot

Stephen King has written some scary books. He is one of the most popular writers alive and millions of people have been terrified by his horror stories. He once said that *I am Legend* was one of the books that inspired him to write. One of his earliest and best-loved novels, *Salem's Lot*, is a vampire novel that was inspired by *Dracula*.

It begins with a man and boy travelling in Mexico. They are not father and son but they are bonded by a terrible experience that has taken place in a town on the east coast of America called Jerusalem's Lot. The novel then returns to the point where the writer arrives in the town. His name is Ben Mears and he lived in the town as a small boy. A frightening experience in an old house overlooking the town has left him with nightmares. He has come back to write a book about the house and hopefully come to terms with the experience. He attempts to rent the old house only to find that it has recently been purchased by a man called Straker and his mysterious silent partner, Barlow. Not long after he arrives, a boy called Danny Glick and his little brother disappear. Danny returns but dies soon after. Strange events begin to take place in the town. A dog is found hanging on the cemetery gates. People are dying and their bodies are disappearing. The local English teacher, Matt Burke, invites a sick friend to stay at his house only to find that the illness is something far more sinister than a cold. He begins to suspect that the small sleepy town that he has lived in all his life has become infested with vampires.

In Bram Stoker's novel, *Dracula*, Van Helsing, the vampire hunter, observes that the 'strength of the vampire is that no one will believe in him'. The teacher Matt Burke has to convince Ben and others that vampires do exist and have arrived in Salem's Lot. It is a tradition in vampire stories that certain characters will find it hard to believe in the existence of vampires. Writers use these characters to represent the reader. We don't believe in vampires and the challenge for the writer is to make us believe in the vampire in the story. *Salem's Lot* is not set in the future or the past but is meant to seem as much like the present as possible. Stephen King builds up the image of a typical American small town with its various characters only to shatter the image by turning many of its citizens into vampires. The suggestion that vampires could come among us without us noticing is an important part of the tradition that goes back to Polidori's Lord Ruthven. It remains a component of contemporary stories such as *Twilight*.

Like *I am Legend*, the vampires eventually outnumber the humans in the town, leaving a handful of characters in serious danger. The vampires take over the town but not before a boy, Mark, destroys Barlow. The story ends where it began, with Ben and the boy, Mark, heading back to Salem's Lot to begin the battle again.

Interview with the Vampire

Stephen King's story is one of his most popular and remains an important part of the vampire tradition. It is, however, overshadowed somewhat by a book that appeared only six months later, in April of 1976. Anne Rice's *Interview with the Vampire* was probably the most influential vampire novel since *Dracula*. It spawned many sequels and a film of questionable quality, but began a new chapter in the story of the vampire and is probably the starting point of its current popularity.

The story begins in the present with a vampire, Louis, preparing to give an interview to a young reporter. He tells him about how he became a vampire two hundred years earlier when he was attacked by a vampire called Lestat. The story follows Louis as he struggles with his new identity in the face of the vicious Lestat. *Twilight* fans will recognize something of Edward in Louis. As Lestat kills human after human, Louis subsists on the blood of animals. The story develops as Louis tries to destroy Lestat and then leaves for Europe to make contact with other vampires. The first that he meets in Eastern Europe are zombies that have been brought back to life. It is an echo of the earliest vampire legends from that part of the world.

Louis, and his companion Claudia, a child vampire, finally end up in Paris where they once again encounter Lestat, along with a group of vampires who reside in a theatre. Here he meets Armand who becomes his companion after Claudia is killed.

Where *Salem's Lot* followed Bram Stoker's template and focussed on the vampire hunters rather than the vampire, Anne Rice dispenses with any kind of traditional Van Helsing or Jonathan Harker characters. In some sense, Louis is, at once, both the hunter and the hunted. If Lestat is the Dracula figure in *Interview with the Vampire*, then Louis becomes Van Helsing. He seeks to destroy a vampire but at the same time has to come to terms with the fact that he is one himself. It isn't a new idea by any means. Varney was a reluctant vampire in the 1840s. But for contemporary writers it moved the story out of the traditional horror or science fiction domain. *Interview with the Vampire* and its sequels are not books about monsters. Rice uses the vampire story in a manner that combines historical fiction, crime, and the occult to create a new kind of tale. Louis is the first in a series of vampires with human feelings. Though the TV vampire, Barnabas Collins, may be model for Louis, Anne Rice turned the sensitive undead man into a literary phenomenon. A new era of romantic vampire stories had begun.

And in 2002 a woman in Phoenix, Arizona, had a dream about a girl and her sparkling vampire lover. Almost two hundred years after another young woman had a dream that created the literary sensation of *Frankenstein*, Stephenie Meyer used her dream as the basis for her first novel, *Twilight*.

Twilight

Meyer's dream was of two people in a meadow. They are in love, but there are complications. She is a normal girl and he, in Meyer's words, is 'fantastically beautiful, sparkly — and a vampire'. This sparkly vampire is having a lot of trouble restraining himself from killing the girl. The dream had such a profound effect on Meyer that she found herself compelled to get it down on paper. She reports that she wrote mostly at night after her children were asleep, sometimes producing only a page or two and sometimes producing an entire chapter.

While the *Twilight* series features certain vampire traditions, Meyer's influences were not vampire stories. In fact, she has said repeatedly that she deliberately avoided the genre to ensure that her story was original. So what are her influences? There is a clue in her lead vampire's name. Edward Rochester is the dark hero of Charlotte Bronte's classic novel, *Jane Eyre*. This book appeared in 1847, at about the same time that readers were being terrified by *Varney the Vampire*. Bronte's book is not, in any sense, a vampire novel. However, it does make use of the Gothic images and ideas that are so much a component of the vampire genre.

It is a tale of a young orphan, Jane, and her adventures in various households. Eventually, she ends up as a governess in a large old house called Thornfield Manor. The owner of the manor is Edward Rochester, a moody, mysterious, and much older man, who slowly grows close to Jane. However, the manor seems to be haunted by some kind of malevolent spirit. This spirit turns out to Edward's wife, who has gone mad and been locked away. Jane only finds out about her on the day she is to be married to Edward. The wedding plans are scuttled and Jane is once again on her own. Eventually she finds her way back to Rochester after he is badly injured in a fire that finally kills his mad wife.

Jane Eyre remains one of the most popular and influential novels of all time. The key to its appeal is the combination of romance and Gothic horror. Countless writers and filmmakers have been inspired by the relationship that develops between Jane and Rochester. It is not surprising that Stephenie Meyer found something that she could use in her story.

Vampire aficionados, however, haven't been universally convinced by *Twilight*'s portrayal of their creature. For many, a sparkling vampire is nowhere near frightening enough to rate in the pantheon of the undead. They feel that Edward's vampirism is superficial and simply a plot device without any real attention to detail or the long vampire tradition. These criticisms seem unfair when one considers the tradition itself. The vampire has never stopped changing. Every writer recreates the creature to suit their own purposes. Intriguingly, the one element that has remained consistent is the idea of the 'outsider', and this is certainly part of Meyer's tale. One way of reading vampire stories is to see them as being about how we, as human beings, deal with those who are different from us. Edward Cullen and his family live on the edge of the town and are regarded in much the same manner as Barstow in *Salem's Lot*, the young vampires in *The Lost Boys*, and Anne Rice's fringe-dwelling Lestat. Edward is also part of a tradition of vampires who find themselves forced to live in human society for one reason or another.

It is also fair to say that however the *Twilight* series has been received by vampire fans, it is destined to become one of the key texts in the genre. Already, its influence is clear. Bookstores are overflowing with 'vampire romance' stories, most of which owe a considerable debt to Meyer's creations.

The vampire tale has survived because it is a good story. Fans can decide what kind of vampires they like best, but the diversity of versions is one of the reasons the genre has continued for so long.

THE 1992 NOVEL ANNO DRACULA *by Kim Newman, is arguably one of the cleverest vampire stories ever written. The story is a steam-punk style alternative history set in the nineteenth century. Count Dracula has married Queen Victoria and England is a police state where vampires run the show. But Jack the Ripper is murdering vampire prostitutes and he must be stopped! The cast of characters is enormous and involves figures from the past 200 years of vampire stories including Kurt Barlow from* Salem's Lot, *Varney the Vampire, Barnabas Collins from* Dark Shadows *and Kolchak from* The Night Stalker *television show. Many of the characters from Bram Stoker's original novel appear as well. As a result,* Anno Dracula *is both an entertaining novel and a surreal history of the genre.*

Epilogue

THERE AREN'T MANY THINGS that are certain in the entertainment world, but the appearance of a vampire film, book, comic, or television show is guaranteed. Since the beginning of cinema, not a year has passed in which something resembling a vampire film has not appeared in theatres. Similarly, vampire novels have been selling steadily for almost 200 years. Only when comic-book publishers themselves decided to ban the creature did vampires disappear from comic books. Television's relationship with the undead has been somewhat less certain but very few seasons have gone by in the last 50 years without at least one vampire making an appearance.

But the question that people often ask is: why? Why don't we get tired of these creatures? Lots of popular characters have disappeared from the public consciousness. Vampires aren't going anywhere.

One simple explanation is the versatility of the vampire character. They need blood to live and they are 'undead'. Once these two items are established, the vampire can be whatever the writer wants them to be, and fit them into whatever kind of story they wish to tell. Cowboy vampires, space vampires and child vampires are just some of the countless variations on the theme. Vampires work as well in romance stories as they do in detective stories. Science-fiction writers have focussed on the nature of their condition and fantasy writers have found ways of working them into the elaborate otherworlds of their fiction. A vampire, unlike, say, Godzilla, can be a low-key minor character, or a figure of sympathy. Women can fall in love with the debonair and regal Dracula figure while men can be mesmerised by the attentions of the female vampire. Unlike Frankenstein, the other character to emerge from that story night in

Geneva, vampires can move among us quite easily. Werewolves, once the full moon hits, are just rabid dogs. Poltergeists can only cause havoc for the people they haunt. A vampire might, as Wynona Ryder finds out, offer a candlelit dinner before sinking the teeth in. The vampire can be a civilised monster, and we are fascinated by those types.

Our interest in them is, like most things, an interest in ourselves. As human beings, we spend a lot of time defining ourselves by what we are not. We are not orangutans although we aren't far off. Our fear that these creatures will disappear may be, in part, a fear that they will no longer be here to be different from us. The history of vampire stories suggests a similar impulse. John Polidori's Lord Ruthven was almost certainly based on Lord Byron, a man sometimes called the first celebrity. Byron's scandalous life was the subject of gossip in England for decades. He was a man, and a member of the aristocracy, but his behaviour set him apart. He was fascinating because, despite appearances, he was different. It makes sense then that the first celebrity is also the model for the first modern vampire.

By the time Bram Stoker wrote *Dracula*, the

British Empire was at its most powerful and England was coming to terms with the reality of the people who lived in its colonies. Colonialism isn't simply a conquest of a foreign nation. A successful colony means that there is some exchange of views and cultural traditions. England changed India but India changed England. Count Dracula's foreignness is as important as the fact that he is a vampire. His arrival in England would have resonated with Stoker's readers who were beginning to see different faces and hear different languages on the streets of London.

In the 1950s in the wake of the nuclear bombing of Nagasaki and Hiroshima at the end of the Second World War, vampires were sometimes portrayed as post-apocalyptic creatures. The fear of how nuclear and chemical warfare could change us is played out in these stories. In the late sixties, as feminism took hold, female vampires became popular again. The vampire has been used in the same way that other stories have been used since the beginning of civilisation. What we don't understand or fear can form the basis for a vampire story. Stephen King's *Salem's Lot* appeared in a time when American society was changing very quickly. The small New England town that is completely transformed within a matter of weeks would have resonated with a population trying to understand who they were in the wake of the Vietnam War.

I have only touched on a small number of the many vampire books, films, television shows and comics that have appeared in the past 200 years. Some readers may be shocked at the omission of their particular favourite story or wonder why on earth I would have included something like *The Munsters*. Books like this will always challenge notions of something as wide and varied as vampire stories. But if you keep reading and viewing, you will be able to make up your own mind. If you haven't read Bram Stoker's *Dracula*, I highly recommend picking up a copy of this classic. Sheridan Le Fanu's *Carmilla* is more difficult for modern readers, but it will surprise you if you haven't read it. Richard Matheson's *I am Legend* digs deep into the idea of vampires and vampirism. Rent some of the old vampire movies. The special effects are laughable and the acting may be a little stiff, but in *Nosferatu* and the original Bela Lugosi

Dracula you will see where it all began. Both of them are pretty scary too! But don't stop with my suggestions. There are plenty of vampires out there and you will soon discover the kind that suits you. Read, watch, discuss, and most of all, enjoy!

Required Viewing

10 Classic Vampire Films:

1. *Nosferatu* (1922)
2. *Dracula* (1931)
3. *Dracula's Daughter* (1936)
4. *The Horror of Dracula* (1959)
5. *Fright Night* (1985)
6. *Lost Boys* (1987)
7. *Near Dark* (1987)
8. *Buffy The Vampire Slayer* (1992)
9. *Blade* (1998)
10. *Shadow of a Vampire* (2000)

Honourable Mentions:
Let the Right One In (2009)
Bram Stoker's Dracula (1992)

Required Reading

10 Interesting Vampire Novels:

1. *The Vampyre* by John Polidori (1819)
2. *Carmilla* by Sheridan Le Fanu (1872)
3. *Dracula* by Bram Stoker (1897)
4. *I am Legend* by Richard Matheson (1954)
5. *Salem's Lot* by Stephen King (1975)
6. *Interview with the Vampire* by Anne Rice (1976)
7. *Anno Dracula* by Kim Newman (1992)
8. *Twilight* by Stephenie Meyer (2005)
9. *The Historian* by Elizabeth Kostova (2005)
10. *Let the Right One In* by John Ajvide Lindqvist (English edition 2007)

Required Listening

A bloody playlist, or, stuff the author listened to while writing this book:

Bela Lugosi is Dead by Bauhaus (1979)

I used to go to a dance place called The Voodoo Club in Toronto in the early 1980s. There was a guy there called Zephyr who, it was said, was a vampire. I can remember watching him dance to this song. It made sense.

Psychotic Reaction by The Count Five (1966)

The band dressed like vampires and this three chord garage burner is a rock and roll classic.

It's Monster Surfing Time by The Deadly Ones (1964)

An instrumental with scary monster sounds. The combination of horror and surfing seems unlikely but it works somehow.

Sunglasses After Dark by The Cramps (1980)

The best live band I have ever seen. The lead singer, Lux Interior, and his wife, guitarist Poison Ivy, looked liked lounge vampires. The music was an amazing combination of rockabilly, garage punk, surf, and soul selling Delta Blues. The songs were hilarious but kind of scary too. A band worth hearing.

The Black Angel's Death Song by The Velvet Underground (1967)

While the summer of love was breaking out in San Francisco, this group of New York night creatures dressed in black and played bleak Rock and Roll for people who had no interest in flowers or peace.

Swampland by The Scientists (1982)

An Australian entry, this is perhaps the best-known song by the underrated Kim Salmon and his band The Scientists. It doesn't have anything to do with vampires per se, but I listened to it over and over while I was writing the book. 'In my heart there's a place called Swampland…' I think there might be a few vampires in that place.

Release The Bats by The Birthday Party (1981)

Melbourne's own vampire, Nick Cave, with his pre-Bad Seeds band. This might be a shock to fans of his later work. It is two and half minutes of bass guitar driven, danceable horror. And yes, he is screaming about vampires at the end of the song.

Werewolves of London by Warren Zevon (1978)

Okay, okay, it is a song about werewolves. But listen to the lyrics carefully. 'His hair was perfect.' What kind of werewolf has perfect hair? Lon Chaney is mentioned along with his son. Both of them played vampires. London is Dracula's town too. Case closed. This should be called Vampires of London.

Shadowplay by Joy Division (1979)

Again, there is no real connection with vampires other than the fact that this remains a very creepy song.

The Killing Moon by Echo and the Bunnyman (1984)

Gloriously eerie song that continues to attract new fans; the landscape here is certainly one that could feature vampires.

References

1. Auerbach, Nina; *Our Vampires Ourselves*, Chicago: University of Chicago Press, 1995

2. Farson, Daniel; *The Man Who Wrote Dracula*, London: Michael Joseph, 1975

3. Gelder, Ken; *Reading The Vampire*, London: Routledge, 1994

4. Hadju, David; *The Ten Cent Plague*, New York: Picador, 2008

5. Holmes, Richard; *Shelley: The Pursuit*, London: Flamingo, 1974

6. Melton, J. Gordon; *The Vampire Book*, Detroit: Visible Ink, 1994

7. Seymour, Mary; *Mary Shelley*, London: Picador, 2000

8. Skal, David J.; *Vampires: Encounters With The Undead*, New York: Black Dog and Leventhal, 2006

9. Summers, Montague; *The Vampire*, New York: Dorset Press, 1991

I also used various websites as part of my research. As you might imagine, to search the word 'vampire' is to discover a whole world of odd people, some of whom believe themselves to be vampires. This might sound old-fashioned, but if you would like to know more about the history of vampire legends and stories, books are probably a more reliable choice. Happy vampire hunting!

Index

Acknowledgements

I would like to thank my editor at black dog, Melissa Keil, for her enthusiasm and patience. Hard work and dedication only begin to describe her contribution to this book.

I should also mention my students, past and present, who have listened to my stories and told me a few of their own. Plenty of the material in this book was road tested in my classes. Thank you all for your comments, smiles and nods.

And finally, a big thank you to my mum, Betsy Matheson, who took me to lots of plays when I was little and has been giving me books to read for more than forty years.

About the Author

Tony Thompson is a Melbourne-based writer and teacher. He has written for *The Age* and *The Australian* and taught English in several Melbourne high schools. He is originally from Toronto, Canada, but has lived in Australia for more than fifteen years. In 1988, after finishing his undergraduate degree at Trent University in Peterborough, Ontario, he left for a short backpacking tour of Ireland. This first trip led to years of aimless but interesting rambles in Europe, North America and Asia. In 1992, he took a job teaching English conversation in Tokyo. An evening of karaoke led to a long-term relationship and marriage to an Australian who was also teaching English in Tokyo. In 1994, he and his wife moved to a small flat in Melbourne which seemed quite large after living in Japan. In 2002, he relocated to Borneo where he worked in a large water-village. Amid the monkeys, feral dogs, and students who doubled as smugglers, he taught English and, for the first and final time, Beginner Guitar. Wearying of the long boat ride to work, he returned to Australia where he continues to teach and write. He lives in the western suburbs of Melbourne with his wife and son.

Also by Tony Thompson

A preview of *Shakespeare: The Most Famous Man in London*

CHAPTER ONE: THE CONY-CATCHER

Elizabethan London, or Why Shakespeare's plays are so violent

In one of Shakespeare's early plays, *Titus Andronicus*, a woman has her tongue cut out and her hands chopped off. Later in the play, her father is tricked into chopping off one of his own hands. The play finishes with another woman sitting down to eat a pie made from the bodies of her two sons. *Romeo and Juliet* finishes with a double suicide, completing a play filled with street fights, stabbings and gang violence. *Macbeth* finishes with the main character's head being swung around in victory. Hamlet ends in a massacre that kills nearly every main character.

Most of Shakespeare's plays, even the comedies, contain an element of violence. Was Shakespeare a bloodthirsty maniac? Or was he a shrewd businessman who knew what brought in the crowds? Certainly, in his time as in ours, violence and sex were what people wanted to see. Even so, it is difficult to imagine people having the stomach for the level of violence described above; unless of course, those people lived in a society where violence was part of everyday life. Shakespeare's London is renowned for its cultural life, but there was another side to the city and Shakespeare didn't shy away from it.

Shakespeare left his hometown of Stratford some time between 1585, when he attended the christening of his twins, and 1592, when a rival playwright criticised him in a famous pamphlet. The period in between is sometimes referred to as Shakespeare's 'lost years', and there are numerous theories about what he was up to in this time. In all likelihood, he got fed up with making gloves in his father's workshop and joined one of the many theatre companies that passed through Stratford. By the time he reached London he would have been taking minor roles as an actor, perhaps helping to adapt stories and older plays for performance. Will did not grow up in London, so the impression that the city made on him when he arrived would have left an enduring mark on his imagination.

The Lost Years

In 1585, William Shakespeare signed the baptism certificate for his twin children, Judith and Hamnet. He was twenty-one years old, and had been married to his wife, Anne, for three years. For the next seven years there is no evidence at all as to what he was doing. When he appears again in 1592, it is as a rising playwright in London. This period in Shakespeare's life is known as the 'lost years' and it has produced more speculation than just about anything else in Shakespeare's story. There has been much debate about Shakespeare and the Catholic religion. Some historians who believe that Shakespeare was a secret Catholic might put him among other secret Catholics during this period. Other historians might decide that Shakespeare was a teacher, and have him pressing Latin onto his young charges throughout the late 1580s. Or perhaps, as has been put forward many times, he was a soldier and visited places like Verona, Copenhagen and Venice. Shakespeare's plays reveal all kinds of obscure knowledge on a wide variety of subjects from astronomy to botany to music. There is always something in the plays that can be used to support a claim about these 'lost years'. The witty gravedigger in *Hamlet* might be based on Shakespeare's own experiences in this profession. He may have been a gatekeeper like the fellow who answers the endless knocking in *Macbeth*. Perhaps, he was a money-lender like Shylock in *The Merchant of Venice*. The most famous story is that he was caught poaching deer and driven out of Stratford. This myth began not long after he died but is not well supported by any surviving evidence.

Sometimes it is easier to simply draw a line from point A to B and then determine the straightest path. How does a person become a playwright? They get involved with the theatre. How do they become involved with the theatre? They start as a stagehand or helper or as an actor of bit parts. There is plenty of evidence that Shakespeare acted in plays during the 1590s. It would make sense that he began as an actor and slowly developed his skills as a playwright. There are numerous references to acting and actors in his plays. In Hamlet, the title character gives detailed instructions on acting to a group of players. Now this may seem like the same trap as deciding that he was a gravedigger, but the line between actor and playwright is straighter than most of the other possibilities.

The 'lost years' will continue to tantalise historians and biographers forever unless a diary or a lost bundle of letters turns up to solve the mystery.

In Shakespeare's time, much of the population of London was drunk. Drinking beer was relatively safe in a city where drinking the polluted water could be suicide. The main source of drinking water, the River Thames, was filled with dead animals, human waste and garbage. So children, adults and old people drank beer. They drank it morning, noon and night. There is no shortage of drunks in Shakespeare's plays either. Falstaff, the Gatekeeper in *Macbeth* and Sir Toby Belch in *Twelfth Night* are just some of the comical figures associated with alcohol in his work. Not surprisingly, Londoners in Shakespeare's time were also great singers who sang the popular songs of the day as they went about their business. Most of Shakespeare's plays feature songs, which would have been quite significant to the original audiences. If they liked the song, they would buy the lyrics and learn them. There was no recorded music in this period, so if you liked a song, you sang it.

But drinking didn't just produce jolly singers. In a city of 150 000, where beer was being drunk in large amounts, street brawls were common. Arguments could quickly get out of hand, for as well as being very drunk, Londoners in Shakespeare's time were also very well armed. The city had a vast criminal class and there was no real police force. Citizens had to take responsibility for their own protection. Most carried a rapier, along with a dagger and possibly another concealed knife. A fight that started between two people often drew in others, and sometimes developed into a riot. By some estimates, there were more than thirty major riots in London between 1580 and 1600 — more than one a year. There is a flavour of this in *Romeo and Juliet*. The opening scene sees a humorous exchange of insults flare up into a battle between two families. The Prince breaks it up, noting that three brawls 'have thrice disturbed the quiet of our streets'. Soon after, Romeo wearily asks his cousin, Benvolio, 'What fray was here? Oh tell me not for I have heard it all.' Shakespeare's original audience might have sympathised.

Shakespeare may have also felt he had to compete

with the other main form of entertainment at the time. Bear baiting was hugely popular, and Shakespeare must have noted the high level of cruelty and violence in this terrifying 'sport'. A bear was tied to a post and attacked by dogs. The bear either killed the dogs or was killed by them. Generally the bear would win, but not without sustaining horrible injuries. Sometimes the bear was blinded to even the odds. On at least one occasion a blinded bear broke loose, causing pandemonium among the spectators.

Some of the bears became celebrities. A bear named Harry Hunks is regularly mentioned by Elizabethan writers, and another, Sackerson, is referred to by Shakespeare in *The Merry Wives of Windsor*.

In *King Lear*, a character named Gloucester is being held by Lear's two evil daughters. He says, 'I am tied to th' stake, and I must stand the course.' Soon after this reference to bear baiting, Gloucester is blinded in a moment of incredible cruelty. Clearly, Shakespeare had bear baiting in mind for this scene. The other famous reference is a stage direction in *The Winter's Tale*. 'Exit, pursued by bear' is how a character called Antigonus leaves the stage. Presumably, the 'bear' would have been an actor dressed in a costume rather than Sackerson or Harry Hunks themselves. Shakespeare wasn't going to risk being upstaged by a rival celebrity! *King Lear* also makes reference to another popular sport of the time. Early in the play, Lear himself says, 'Nor tripped neither, you base football player.' There is another mention of football in a play called *A Comedy of Errors*.

What kind of football was played in Shakespeare's time? The most common version, sometimes called Gameball or Mob Football, was played on Sundays. The goals were kilometres apart in different parts of the city and the objective was to keep possession of the ball. There was a myth that Gameball had once been played with the heads of traitors, but the ball was typically made of rough leather or a pig's bladder. The teams were enormous and there was no rougher sport in Elizabethan England (unless, of course, you were a bear). As the ball moved around the streets, fights broke out, old scores were settled and shops were looted. Spectators pelted the players with rotten vegetables. One writer of the time observed that the game, 'was more a kind of fight than play or recreation, a bloody and murdering practice than a fellowly sport or pastime'. He was probably right. This kind of football is still played once a year in a town called Ashbourne in Derbyshire, England. It remains a very rough game.

When the residents of Shakespeare's London weren't engaging in drunken brawls, watching bears battle with dogs or footballers breaking bones, they were probably watching a public execution.

The worst crime that a person could commit was treason. To speak or plot against the Queen was the surest path to a slow, horrible and very public death. A treasonous citizen could look forward to being dragged through the streets to an execution site. There, several possible punishments awaited. The prisoner might be hanged; dropped slowly so that he eventually suffocated. The executioner, as a bonus, might cut out the prisoner's heart and show it to the crowd. The other possibility was being drawn and quartered while still alive, and having one's body parts thrown into a fire. The prisoner's head would then be stuck on a gate to feed the large black ravens of London, providing a vivid warning to anyone else pondering treason. On a daily basis, Londoners would see their fellow citizens being whipped, beaten or placed in the stocks for a variety of offences. Sometimes prisoners were chained to a wall below the waterline in the filthy River Thames so that when the tide came in they were nearly drowned.

Cony-Catchers, Cozening and the London Underworld

'Cony-catching' and 'cozening' were Elizabethan terms for tricking someone in order to rob them. People were 'gulled' or 'cozened' by elaborate schemes devised by criminals. Many of Shakespeare's plays involved plots or subplots where people are fooled by others. *Othello*, *Much Ado About Nothing* and *Twelfth Night*, along with others, feature a character or characters who are comprehensively deceived. The vast criminal network that existed in Shakespeare's London inspired its own literature. Shakespeare's sometime nemesis, Robert Greene, wrote several pamphlets on the subject. The appetite for stories of criminals like the notorious Cutting Ball was large, and Shakespeare found ways to incorporate them into his plays. *Henry IV* is an historical play about an English king, but some of the secondary characters, such as Falstaff and his criminal gang, are far more interesting.

It would have been almost impossible for a Londoner to avoid the rougher elements of life in their city. Shakespeare sought to catch the interest of playgoers by offering them great stories and interesting characters speaking witty or thought-provoking dialogue. But he also tried to show them something of themselves and the world they lived in. So in a city like London he could hardly ignore violence.

Elizabethan London

London grew and flourished during this period. The population rose above 200 000 as immigrants from war-torn Europe flooded in. New neighbourhoods began to develop and sprawl outwards from the city, but most of the population lived within the city walls. The incredible density of people in such a small area meant that disease spread quickly. It was in this period that London became an increasingly important centre for trade, which made for a busy city but also one where the gap between rich and poor grew. The first maps of London were drawn in this period.

Queen Elizabeth

Shakespeare is often associated with 'Elizabethan' England. Elizabeth Tudor became Queen of England in 1558 upon the death of her older half-sister, Queen Mary, also known as 'Bloody Mary'. Elizabeth was the daughter of Henry VIII and his second wife, Anne Boleyn. Her reign lasted more than forty years. Elizabeth enjoyed the arts and saw many of Shakespeare's plays performed at Whitehall palace.